TRANSFORM
THRIVE

The Guide to Business Evolution and Success

Jheeva Subramanian

Edited by Dinesh Sandhu

Table Of Contents

01

Introduction

One of the hottest topics that is engulfing almost all industries is Transformation (either a complete business transformation or digital transformation). It is a topic that I find very intriguing and also very excited to be part of. The topic usually garners various views, opinions, and varying degrees of understanding of what transformation entails, especially digital transformation. There are no right or wrong answers as it can mean different things to different people.

It is an expansive topic and there are many factors that should be considered before an organisation undertakes its transformation journey. In this book, I cover some of the concepts that I believe are important in a transformation journey of a business.

I spent the last three years engineering the transformation of a very dated department store chain in Singapore and the learnings from that project have taught me a lot on what to do and, more importantly, what not to do. I have also included some real-life case studies to give an example of how the concepts are implemented and their outcomes. In my effort to transform the business, I spent a lot of time speaking to many consultants, C-suite professionals, and industry experts. Having spoken to many of them, I generally find that the understanding of 'digital transformation' can be summarised into four categories.

Sceptics – People who still do not believe that there is a need to digitally transform. Hard to believe this, right? But I assure you that I still find some businesses that are reluctant to embark on any type of change.

Online presence – Secondly, people who define it as 'going on-line'; as in having an E-commerce platform, marketplace presence and having presence in social media channels.

Use of digital technologies – The third group, in addition to having an online presence, talks about the technology needed to merge the online and offline offering, the importance of data, the use of artificial intelligence and machine learning, change in mindset and culture, etc.

Different view – The final group, and the group that I subscribe to talks about everything that the third group believes in and, on top of that, stresses the point of new business models. This group takes into consideration how they use technology to improve processes internally, add value to their customers and how to leverage the experience and insights to evolve into a new business model or add a new revenue stream.

To be clear, I am not saying that any of the above groups beliefs are right or wrong. There are various opinions on the topic, and I have simply categorised them into four categories.

Although it is widely acknowledged that businesses must undergo transformation, creating a plan and implementing it can be challenging for many. Beginning the process may seem daunting; the aim of this book is to provide learnings from what I have experienced and key concepts that I believe you should consider when devising your transformation strategy. It covers various topics from recognising the necessity for change to identifying important concepts crucial in formulating effective strategies. Use this as a starting point and customise accordingly to align the plan with your organisation's objectives and ambitions.

This book delves into different areas of transformation and presents actionable tips for success. Chapter 2 examines the reasons why transformation is necessary, while also highlighting the factors that contribute to its urgency. Chapter 3 emphasises how crucial experimentation and innovation are in propelling a successful transformation process.

Meanwhile, Chapter 4 centres on technology's role in driving change, with Chapter 5 exploring how businesses can benefit from adopting platforms as their business model as part of their transformation strategy.

The sixth chapter highlights the crucial significance of individuals in driving the transformation process, while the seven chapter promotes a Lean and Agile methodology for this undertaking. Chapter 8 covers co-creation and ecosystems' relevance to such transformations, whereas Chapter 9 underscores how imperative it is to have a distinct strategy that guides all change efforts.

The tenth chapter concentrates on establishing fresh business models as an outcome of these modifications. Chapter 11 emphasises the necessity of ongoing reinvention amidst ever-evolving commercial circumstances. Chapter 12 takes stock of forthcoming trends likely to shape future business landscapes driven by continuous transformation initiatives.

Chapter 13 offers a tangible illustration of how retail companies can implement transformation strategies in real-world scenarios. Lastly, Chapter 14 details a specific instance when such efforts were executed.

In summary, this book emphasises that transformation is essential for organisations to survive and expand. The core message highlights the crucial factors businesses need to bear in mind while commencing their transformational journey. By incorporating the concepts and strategies presented in this book, companies can flourish amidst a constantly evolving business landscape and set themselves up for future triumphs.

Digital Transformation

Let's start with a definition of "Digital Transformation" - digital transformation is the process of using digital technologies to fundamentally change how a business operates and **delivers value to its customers**.

Now, you might be thinking, 'Okay, that sounds simple enough. But why is it important for companies to digitally transform?' The answer lies in the rapidly changing business landscape. Technology is playing an increasingly larger role in shaping the way we live, work, and communicate, and companies that do not embrace digital transformation risk falling behind their competitors who are already leveraging digital technologies to improve their operations and customer experiences.

So, what does digital transformation actually involve? Well, it is not just about going online or investing in technology. Digital transformation is a much more comprehensive process that involves rethinking and redesigning business processes, customer experiences, design thinking, class-leading UI/UX and even entire business models to take full advantage of new digital capabilities.

> **"There is no alternative to digital transformation. Visionary companies will carve out new strategic options for themselves – those that don't adapt will fail"**
>
> - Jeff Bezos, Amazon

Some of the technology-driven initiatives that have the potential to transform the way a business operates, from streamlining internal processes to delivering a more personalised customer experience include cloud computing, big data analytics, artificial intelligence, ESG goals and the Internet of Things (IoT) and will be part of the digital transformation effort.

One of the most crucial aspects of digital transformation is the importance of people, culture and leadership. The integration of digital technology into a business requires a change in mindset and new leadership skills to effectively lead and manage the workforce in this digital era. This is why it is extremely crucial for companies to have a strong human capital strategy in place if they want to succeed in their digital transformation efforts. Chapter 6 is dedicated to People.

Another important aspect of digital transformation is the role of co-creation and ecosystems. Companies that embrace open innovation and work closely with their partners and customers to co-create solutions are more likely to succeed in their digital transformation efforts than those that do not. Chapter 8 explains what this means and how to go about implanting this strategy.

So, as you can see, digital transformation is much more than just going online or investing in technology. It is a comprehensive effort that requires a change of mindset, new leadership skills, and a focus on co-creation and ecosystems among other concepts.

To remain competitive in today's rapidly evolving digital era, digital transformation is an essential process for all companies regardless of industry. By embracing digital technologies and rethinking the way they operate, companies can improve their performance, better serve their customers, and remain relevant in a rapidly changing business landscape.

The risk of not transforming can be disastrous. Even if your company is currently the leader in the industry and even if there are no present competitors in the market to cause any harm to your business, there is a very high possibility that a start-up is working behind the scenes to disrupt your business model. Chapter 2 will demonstrate a real-life example of how this has manifested.

This book will outline what I believe are concepts and best practices for wanting to transform. We will discuss the importance of people and leadership, the role of co-creation and ecosystems, how to define and implement digital transformation strategies, and much more.

I sincerely hope that it will help in your transformation journey.

02

The Need to Transform

I would like to start by showing you a case study that illustrates what happens when you ignore the need to change. It is like driving a car without ever changing the oil. Eventually, the engine will break down and you will not be able to go anywhere.

Blockbuster

David Cook, who founded Blockbuster had previously worked in the oil and gas industry providing computer software services. He saw the potential in the video rental business, which led him to open the first Blockbuster store in 1985 and then three more stores the next year. Blockbuster was not only a film rental store, they also offered video game rentals and even sold music. It was very popular in the 90s when VHS was the leading format to watch movies on videos.

Blockbuster dominated the entertainment industry but is now a distant memory for most people. It closed all of its corporate-owned stores by 2014, leaving just 50 franchise locations. Four years later, it had only one outlet left in America, and in 2019, when Blockbuster shut its last outpost in Australia, it became the last one worldwide. Blockbuster's decline and eventual bankruptcy was a result of its inability to adapt to the digital revolution that was rapidly transforming the way people consumed media. The company's inability to recognise the importance of digital transformation ultimately led to its downfall.

Let's go back to the early 2000s, when Blockbuster was at the height of its success. There were Blockbuster stores everywhere, and the company was a household name. People would visit Blockbuster, mainly on a Friday night to rent the latest movies and video games. It was a ritual for many families, and Blockbuster was considered the king of the video rental industry. I certainly remember my wife and me walking down to our local Blockbuster in Southgate, London, ambling up and down the aisles of the store in search of a movie to rent!

However, the rise of digital technology and the internet was about to disrupt Blockbuster's dominance. As technology advanced and internet speeds increased, more and more people began turning to online services for their entertainment needs. Early companies like Megaupload, Bittorrent drove the internet content revolution followed by Netflix, Amazon and Spotify that democratised visual and audio content. They offered customers the ability to stream movies and TV shows directly to their devices, eliminating the need to leave their homes to visit a physical store.

Blockbuster was slow to recognise the impact that digital technology was having on the entertainment industry. The company continued to focus on its physical stores, investing in new locations and expanding its DVD rental business. Blockbuster's management believed that the company's brick-and-mortar presence was its biggest asset, and that people would always prefer the convenience of visiting a physical store over renting a movie online. Little did they know that eventually people would rather stay at home, slouch on the couch in their sweatpants and watch a movie, than leave the house to rent a DVD.

There was no apparent competitor to Blockbuster at that time, which was probably the reason why Blockbuster rested on their laurels. However, a new startup, Netflix was quick to embrace the concept of digital transformation and soon started becoming a threat to Blockbuster. Netflix pivoted from a DVD rental-by-mail service to an over-the-top (OTT) streaming platform, allowing customers to watch movies and TV shows online. This transition led Netflix to reach a much wider audience, as people no longer had to leave their homes to rent a movie. The company's subscription-based model also made it more convenient for customers, as they could watch as many movies as they wanted for one low monthly fee.

Despite the clear shift in consumer behaviour, Blockbuster continued to resist change. The company dismissed the importance of online streaming and refused to invest in digital technology. Blockbuster management believed that the company's physical stores were its biggest asset, and that people would always prefer visiting a physical store over renting a movie online. Due to Blockbuster's refusal to embrace digital transformation, its customer base dwindled as more and more people switched to streaming services. Brick-and-mortar stores became less relevant, and Blockbuster closed hundreds of stores because of its inability to adapt.

It ended up going bankrupt in 2013.

Netflix

Founded as a DVD rental service in the late 1990s, Netflix pivoted quickly to embrace online streaming. Recognising the potential of digital technology early on and embracing it allowed the company to stay ahead of the curve and eventually overtake Blockbuster as the leading entertainment provider.

In 2007, Netflix launched its streaming platform, which let customers watch movies and TV shows on their TVs directly. The company was willing to make a change and experimented with new technologies. At the beginning, this move was a gamble because internet speeds were not fast enough to support high-quality streaming. However, technology improved, and more people took to online streaming. This move can be compared to playing a game of high-stakes poker: the company bet big with no guarantees that the bet would pay off, but in the end, it was a winning hand.

Another factor that contributed to Netflix's success was its subscription-based business model. Unlike Blockbuster, which relied on customers visiting physical stores to rent DVDs, Netflix offered its customers the ability to watch as many movies and TV shows as they wanted for a low monthly fee. This made Netflix more convenient and cost-effective for customers, as they could watch as much as they wanted without having to leave their homes or pay for each individual rental.

Blockbuster also charged its customers $1 per day for late returns of a DVD which could double or even triple the cost of watching a movie. In 2000, Blockbuster raked in $800 million in late fees, representing 16% of its revenue which is a lot of money to make from people being forgetful – it was almost like Blockbuster decided to give their customers a 'late fee surprise party' every time they returned a movie.

Netflix sets itself apart from its competitors, including Blockbuster, with its focus on innovation and customer convenience. Netflix embraced change and took risks to stay ahead of the curve, while Blockbuster resisted investing in digital technology, despite the impact of digital technology on the entertainment industry.

Customer experience was also a major factor for rise in popularity of Netflix. Netflix's recommendation engine which suggests movies and TV shows based on its customers' viewing history, made it stand out. Netflix used AI based algorithm to keep its customers engaged and loyal to the platform by personalising their entertainment experience. The algorithm determines additional content similar to the content the member has chosen to watch and then reverts to the content that is the most similar to the content that the member has consumed.

Netflix's success in the entertainment industry was not limited to its streaming platform. The company also began producing its own content, including hit shows like 'Stranger Things' and 'The Crown' which allowed Netflix to differentiate itself from its competitors and offer a unique and diverse selection of content that was not available anywhere else.

The rise of Netflix and its eventual dominance in the entertainment industry can be seen as a direct result of Blockbuster's inability to adapt to the digital revolution. Blockbuster's refusal to embrace change and invest in digital technology ultimately led to its downfall, while Netflix's willingness to embrace change and take risks allowed it to become the leading provider of entertainment. In a fast-paced and ever-changing business environment, staying ahead of the curve and embracing new technologies is key to staying relevant and competitive. Netflix's success in an important reminder of this.

The Blockbuster and Netflix stories are classic examples of the winners and losers of the digital revolution, and they are cautionary tales for companies that resist change. Blockbuster, for example, could have embraced online streaming technology and changed its business model, but it opted to remain focused on in-store rentals, ultimately leading to its downfall. Netflix generated $31.6 billion in revenue in 2022.

The Blockbuster and Netflix case study highlights the importance of transformation in the business world. Failure to transform can lead to irrelevance and ultimately, failure. As technology continues to advance at an unprecedented rate, businesses must be willing to adapt and transform to keep pace with changing customer needs and preferences. Those that do not risk falling behind and becoming irrelevant. Not undergoing transformation can be risky as it may lead to businesses becoming too content with the current state of affairs. Such complacency could result in overlooking the necessity for change until it is too late, just like Blockbuster did by prioritising its physical stores and ignoring the potential of online streaming until later.

If businesses fail to innovate, they run the risk of becoming overly dependent on their current customers. Despite changing market conditions, some companies assume that customer loyalty will always endure. However, as evidenced by Blockbuster's demise, this is not necessarily true. Neglecting to adjust to evolving consumer demands puts a business at risk of losing its clients to more creative rivals. For those who do wish to transform, I hope that this book helps in providing you with a guide of what you need to be looking into when planning your organisation's transformation.

In 2000, the CEO of Blockbuster Video had the chance to buy Netflix for $50m. After months of trying to arrange a meeting, Netflix heard back from Blockbuster. Blockbuster agreed to the meeting but was unimpressed during the meeting.

'The dot-com hysteria is completely overblown,' Blockbuster CEO, John Antioco told Netflix. His adviser, Ed Stead, concurred, explaining imperiously that online businesses – still a new phenomenon in 2000 – were not sustainable.

John Antioco was struggling not to laugh when Netflix CEO, John Hastings said, 'Fifty million' when asked what number were they talking about, if Blockbuster was to purchase Netflix. Today Netflix takes in almost $30bn per year in revenue, and Blockbuster is no more!

03

Experimentation & Innovation

Now that we have understood the need and urgency for businesses to transform so as to stay competitive, let us start exploring the concepts that should be included in your transformation journey, starting with the culture and mindset that is needed to ensure that the organisation is ready to embrace a transformation journey: 'Experimentation and Innovation'.

In most cases, managers in businesses use existing data to predict how customers will react to new innovations. They usually end up misinterpreting statistical noise as causality. To find out if a truly innovative idea will succeed, you must put it to the test based on scientific and statistical principles. This is where the concept of experimentation comes in.

Experimentation is about learning. Most breakthrough ideas come about as a result of experimenting. It is about gathering data. Experimentation helps us to make more informed decisions about our ideas and projects. In today's ever evolving business landscape, it is absolutely vital for companies to embrace the concept of experimentation. It allows organisations to try out new ideas, technologies, and approaches in a controlled and safe environment.

Experimentation is a relatively simple concept (We just tend to think that it is complicated!). Companies can test different ideas and technologies to determine which one's work and have the best potential for success, instead of committing a lot of time and resources to a single approach or solution. By using real data and results, organisations can reduce the risk of failure. Experimentation allows companies to develop new products, services and features faster and with lower costs. For instance, a simple example of experimentation is where a company may test different versions of a web page to identify which one has the highest conversion rate, or a business may offer different discounts in different regions to determine which one results in more sales.

Staying relevant and competitive in the industry is important for any business. By continuously experimenting and innovating, it allows a business to stay ahead of the curve as it will be able to identify new trends and technologies early on. This enables the company to quickly adapt to changes in the market. This is one of the key benefits of experimentation.

Innovation is another benefit of experimentation, as experimentation fosters innovation. Let us first understand the meaning of innovation. Most people think innovation is about new ideas: as long as we have ideas, everything else will be solved. Innovation is usually associated with brainstorming sessions with colourful post-it notes. However, it is much more than that. Innovation is defined as - **The process of translating an idea or invention into a good or service that creates value or for which customers will pay**. To be called an innovation, an idea must be replicable at an economical cost and must satisfy a specific need. Although searching for novel ideas is part of innovation and the process, it is not the real challenge or the most challenging part of innovation.

The real challenge is to find a way to execute the idea and make it happen. For instance, a business may have the great idea to develop a product that produces energy from renewable sources, but if it does not have the resources to produce and market the product, the idea will never become an innovation.

When a company builds and encourages a culture of continuous improvement through experimentation and innovation, it allows its employees to think creatively which creates a more efficient, productive, and innovative workforce which can lead to new and better solutions. Unfortunately, this culture is not a norm in most working environments as traditional metrics such as Return on Investments (ROI) often puts a damper on an idea and as a result it never progresses to an experimentation stage. Thus, not realising the potential innovation. Whilst, ROIs should not be ignored, businesses should evaluate ideas based on a few factors and not solely on ROIs.

Relying on gut instincts and assumptions to make decisions, especially when it is made at a 'meeting' formed of a small group of people within the company leads to a high risk of that decision being a wrong decision. Experimentation helps organisations to make data-driven decisions. This helps to reduce the risk of failure and ensures that companies are making informed decisions that are based on real evidence. For instance, running an A/B testing to find out the effectiveness of two different versions of a landing page is more effective rather than a senior manager of the business deciding, 'I like this format and I think customers will like it.'

Despite the apparent benefits of experimentation in business, many organisations are still slow or even reluctant to embrace it. Many organisations still use KPIs that are not effective in measuring performance of an employee and therefore the fear of failure discourages the employees from experimenting. Lack of resources and, also, the lack of understanding of the experimentation process are also reasons why companies do not include experimentation as part of their transformation strategy. To overcome these challenges, companies need to approach experimentation with a clear strategy and a well-defined process. This includes setting clear goals and objectives, defining the scope of the experiment, and establishing metrics for success. Companies should also make sure that they have the resources and expertise to carry out the experiment, including access to the necessary technology and data.

Companies that have a culture that encourages and supports experimentation as part of its DNA, tend to do well in the long run. Educating employees on the importance of experimentation and innovation and ensuring that adequate training and resources are provided is essential. Additionally, companies must reward and recognise employees who participate in experimentation, as this contributes to the development of a culture of innovation and continuous improvement within the organisation.

Microsoft for example, has an 'Innovation Champions' programme that rewards employees who come up with innovative ideas and Google sets aside budgets to reward employees who come up with successful experiments. These companies, as we know them, are role models when it comes to discovering innovative products. They are like the mad scientists of the corporate world, except instead of creating monsters they are creating awesome new products!

Finally, companies need to be prepared for failure. Experimentation can sometimes result in failure, but this should be seen as an opportunity to learn and grow, rather than be viewed as a negative outcome. By accepting failure as a natural part of the experimentation process, companies can reduce the fear of failure and create a culture where it is safe to take risks and try new things. However, it is vital that we learn from the failure. We will cover this concept of 'validated learning' in more detail later in this chapter.

Being Comfortable with Uncertainty

Being uncomfortable with uncertainty is an important element in the culture of experimentation. The pace of change in technology has created an environment that is constantly evolving and becoming increasingly complex and unpredictable. Companies that embrace uncertainty and realise that this mindset is vital for them to instil a culture of experimentation are more likely to succeed.

However, one of the most difficult things to conquer is the mindset of being uncomfortable with uncertainty. C-suite executives and senior managers in companies have in the past always relied on experience and best practices for decision making. For instance, in the past, when planning to invest in a new project, the success or failure of such a project would be determined by considering past investments and their returns. In the digital age, there are often no established best practices, and companies are forced to make decisions based on uncertain information and new data.

Whilst it might sound like an easy concept to adopt and essential for success in the current digital era, in reality, many companies struggle to cultivate this culture in their organisations. This is because it is difficult. It requires everyone in the organisation from the leaders to the customer facing staff member to embrace the unknown and recognise the fact that there is no one right answer to a problem. It requires a culture change to be flexible, open-minded, and willing to take risks. To stay ahead, we need to be able to rapidly identify opportunities, pivot when necessary, and take risks when it makes sense. This requires a certain comfort level with uncertainty and an openness to trying new things.

Experimentation and being comfortable with uncertainty are closely related, and they are both important elements of a digital transformation strategy. As we now know, digital transformation refers to the process of adopting new technologies and processes to improve business operations and customer experiences. These are often driven by experimentation, as companies try new ideas to see what works best and, to be able to do that, they need to be comfortable with uncertainty. It is like a scientist embarking on a new research project, not knowing what the outcome will be. The scientist will need to be comfortable with the unknown, in order to make progress and uncover new insights, and the same is true for digital transformation.

Through experiments, companies can quickly find out what works and what does not work so they can refine their strategy based on new insights. A good strategy is, in the end, a hypothesis about what may work. All business strategies should be tested and refined through a process of disciplined experimentation.

When a company has built a culture of being comfortable with uncertainty, experimentation becomes the norm. Experimentation will allow companies to learn from failure. Failure is an inevitable part of any experimentation process as well as an opportunity to learn and grow. The company could use the information gathered from their mistakes made to improve its products and processes. We will discuss the concept of 'Validated Learning' later in this chapter.

It is imperative that we have a clear understanding of the goals and objectives to ensure successful experimentation as it allows companies to focus their experimentation efforts on areas that are most likely to deliver the results they are looking for. This will also help to ensure that the company is using their resources in the most efficient way.

To summarise, for transformation to be successful, the concept of experimentation is essential. In addition, to encourage a culture of experimentation, we must be comfortable with uncertainty and learn from failed experiments. Organisations can do this by creating an environment that celebrates and rewards the process of experimentation and encourages employees to take calculated risks and learn from the results.

> **'Designing a winning strategy is the art of asking questions, experimenting and then constantly renewing the thinking process by questioning the answers. No matter how good today's strategy is, you must always keep reinventing it.'**
>
> - Constantinos Markides

General Electric (GE)

General Electric (GE) is an example of an organisation that has been at the forefront of experimentation and innovation. GE's commitment to ensuring there is continuing experimentation throughout its organisation has been one of the key factors for its success. It has helped transform GE into a dynamic and thriving organisation. For instance, GE has established a dedicated innovation centre in San Ramon, California, to increase collaboration between engineers, researchers, and product teams to develop new solutions.

There has been a lot of talk about the importance of digital transformation of industries but only a few industrial companies have undertaken the daunting of task of actually committing to transformation. GE has been doing this for over the past 130 years and still is. They have been brilliant on many fronts from innovating light bulbs to industrial automation. GE has been able to maintain its position at the fore by continuing to invest in research and development. They have also been able to build strong relationships with suppliers and customers, which has allowed them to access the most up-to-date technologies and leverage them to improve their operations.

This culture of experimenting and innovating within GE is one of the key reasons for GE's success and longevity. GE has always recognised that it must take risks and experiment to try out new ideas and technologies. It embraces failures, recognising that there are lessons to be learnt from both successful experimentation and failed efforts.

GE's commitment to experimentation has led to an innovative workforce. GE encourages its employees to test new ideas and approaches, which in return creates a culture of continued improvement and the discovery of better solutions. This requires a huge shift in mindset, and GE puts in much effort to nurture such a frame of mind.

In order to effect a transformational shift, GE has embarked on inviting exceptional senior talent from outside the company to move the needle towards its goals more than at any time in its history. It has also increased its employment of women, minorities, and workers from outside the U.S. This has transformed its culture and operating rhythm, choosing speed over bureaucracy. GE has also ensured that everyone in the organisation sees the need for change as existential. We will cover People Strategy in more depth in Chapter 6 which is essential for transformation to take place.

GE relies on the outcomes of experiments to guide its decision making. The company uses real world data and results as a basis for its decisions instead of relying solely on gut instinct and assumptions. Through this process, GE reduces its risk of failure and ensures it is making well-informed decisions. One example of how GE does this is its running of a nine-week experiment which measures the success of a new product before committing to a full launch. This reduces the risk of investing heavily on a project that may not succeed.

GE has also placed importance on ensuring that clear goals and objectives of any experiment are set. Clear scope and metrics for success are established before an experiment is undertaken. This ensures that the experiment is focused and aligned with GE's overall goals and objectives.

A clear example of GE's culture of experimenting and learning its Predix Platform. The platform is the IoT edge-to-cloud foundation shared by GE Digital applications. It supports innovative IoT solutions by providing a common software foundation for fundamental IoT security, scalability, and services functions. The Predix Platform is a cloud-based Platform-as-a-Service (PaaS) for the Industrial Internet.

While there was incremental progress made with the transformation, it never produced the kind of innovation and money that GE had hoped. As a result, the company eventually sold its digital asset business. GE experimented and it did not materialise as expected. They eventually sold that part of the business and moved on.

The reasons for its lack of success are likely complex and multi-faceted, but here are a few key factors that have been reported:

Lack of understanding of customer needs – Predix was designed to be a one-size-fits-all solution, but industrial customers have diverse needs and use cases that require more tailored solutions.

Complexity of implementation – Predix was a complex platform that required significant technical expertise to implement, which made it difficult for many customers to adopt.

Competition from established players – The industrial IoT market was already crowded with established players, and GE faced significant competition from well established companies, such as Siemens and Rockwell Automation.

Slow innovation and development – Predix was slow to develop new features and capabilities, which made it difficult for GE to keep up with meeting the evolving needs of industrial customers.

Poor marketing and branding – Predix was marketed as a platform for industrial IoT, but many customers did not understand what this meant or how it could benefit their operations.

As a result of these challenges, GE has likely learnt the importance of truly understanding customer needs and developing tailored solutions, as well as the need to be in the lead in terms of innovation and development in order to remain competitive. Additionally, GE may have realised the importance of effective marketing and branding to help customers understand the value of its offerings.

In essence, not all experiments work but it is essential that we learn from them and to never stop experimenting. GE has recognised that experimentation can sometimes result in failure, but it takes failure as an opportunity to learn and grow, rather than a negative outcome. GE reduced the fear of failure by creating a culture where it is safe to take risks and try out new things. However, the road to persistent experimentation is not always an easy one. It requires a significant investment of time and resources as well as a willingness to take risks and embrace failure. GE has faced these challenges head-on and has overcome them by approaching experimentation with a clear strategy and a well-defined process.

GE published its Digital Industrial Transformation Playbook, which states:

"Executing a digital industrial transformation strategy can be daunting. As a nearly 130-year-old industrial firm, GE is not immune from the complexity required to implement meaningful change across culture, people, process, and technology. With several years of digital transformation experience under our belt, we've been able to reverse-engineer a repeatable Digital Industrial Transformation Playbook that can be used by our customers and partners to embark on their own transformation journeys".

If you would like a copy of this playbook, please download it from: https://www.protinusgrp.com/post/ge-s-digital-industrial-transformation-playbook.

Validated Learning

Validated learning is a key concept when it comes to experimenting. Obtaining learnings from when an experiment is concluded is extremely important as it helps companies to determine if their experiments are actually providing the results they are looking for, and if not, it allows them to make adjustments and try again. The term was proposed by Eric Ries in 2011 and is used in Scrum. Its defined as 'a unit of progress process and describes conclusions generated by trying out an initial idea and then measuring it against potential customers to validate the effect.'

Using the scientific method to answer questions about market demand is what validated learning does with product development. After the entrepreneur makes a hypothesis about what customers want, he or she builds a prototype or what is referred to as a minimum viable product (MVP). Potential customers are then asked for feedback about the prototype. The information is used to validate reality and fine-tune the product. The process is purposely iterative and is continually repeated throughout the product's lifecycle.

Companies, especially start-ups can greatly benefit from validated learning because it can help them avoid developing features that customers do not want or need. By constantly experimenting and then verifying what matters most to customers, a start-up will be more likely to eventually demonstrate progress against traditional KPIs like revenue. For instance, Amazon famously used validated learning to develop a recommendation engine based on customer purchase data, which helped them increase sales and personalise customer experience.

A typical validated learning process will include the following steps.

Firstly, formulate a hypothesis. A hypothesis is something you believe about your target audience and/or product that needs to be tested. Then devise a metric. A metric is how you measure your hypothesis. Next, conduct the 'experiment.' Finally, analyse the results and make improvements accordingly, and test again.

Testable hypotheses, experiments to test the hypotheses, and analysing the data to evaluate the hypotheses are all part of validated learning. You have real, quantifiable data to back your conclusions up. One simple example of a testable hypothesis is to see if the change in colour of a call-to-action button in a website or email would increase the number of potential customers clicking on it. This experiment would involve changing the colour of the button and tracking the number of customers who have clicked through over a given period of time.

The reason validated learning is so important is that it helps companies to avoid wasting time and resources on experiments that are not likely to deliver the desired results. For example, if a company assumes that a new product will be successful because it has similar features to a competitor's product, they might invest a lot of time and resources into developing and marketing that product. However, if they have not validated this assumption by testing it with customers or through other means, they might be disappointed to find that the product does not sell as well as they had hoped.

The validated learning practice also keeps companies from making assumptions based on limited data or anecdotes. For example, if a company assumes that a new feature is popular because one or two customers had asked for it, they might spend a lot of time and money developing it. They might be disappointed if the feature does not turn out to be as popular as they had hoped because they had not tested it on a larger group of customers.

How do companies obtain data to validate their assumptions and hypothesis? Simple examples are to use customer surveys, user testing, A/B testing or market research. The use of machine learning for predictive analytics is gaining traction but companies need to be careful about the training data: size, period of time, etc. The data collected from these methods gives valuable feedback that companies can use to validate their assumptions and hypothesis which is then used to make data-driven decisions about the best way to proceed with their experiments.

Validated learning also enables companies to test and measure results quickly, allowing them to make more informed decisions and fine-tune their product or service more rapidly than they could through traditional methods.

This iterative approach is vital in the fast-paced world of entrepreneurship and can help entrepreneurs get the best out of their ideas. The iterative process involves repeating a sequence or formula systematically to hone in on the desired result. The process originated as an alternative to the waterfall method for teams to think quickly and respond to issues as they came up. There are five steps in the process: **plan, design, implement, test, and evaluate and review.**

NASA first adopted the iterative model in the 1960s with Project Mercury. They also used it when working with the U.S. Air Force to develop the X-15 hypersonic aircraft. During the 1970s, IBM applied the approach to computer system design.

When done properly and ingrained in the culture of a company, validated learning can also play an important role is building trust with customers. When a company shows that they are committed to providing the best possible products or services by showing that they are creating and improving their product and/or services based on data and feedback from customers, it builds credibility.

Building trust and credibility is a key factor in establishing a long-term successful business. For instance, a car manufacturer that regularly surveys its customers on their experience with the car and uses the data to improve the design of the car or its performance, will build trust with its customers over time and assure them that it is committed to producing the best product.

It is important to understand that the concept of validated learning is not about rationalising failure or telling a good story to hide it. It is about demonstrating progress when we are embedded in uncertainty, and how companies and start-ups grow. A validation learning team proves empirically that they have found valuable facts about a business prospect now and in the future.

The focus of validated learning is on making measurable progress while navigating uncertainty and discovering valuable insights, rather than retrospectively attempting to justify a failure or spin a positive narrative.

In a nutshell, as part of a transformation journey, instilling the mindset and culture of experimentation (which leads to innovation) with validated learning, companies can make more informed decisions based on real life data, iterate and be able adapt quickly to changes and build trust and credibility with their customers. This applies to start-ups and large corporations alike. On the other hand, some people argue that a culture of experimentation can lead to a culture of fear, where employees are constantly second-guessing themselves and their decisions.

This can lead to a feeling of insecurity and a lack of trust in the company's leadership. We address this in the People chapter in this book as it is down to the leadership team to create the right environment to ensure that employees feel safe, comfortable and more importantly motivated to embrace these concepts.

Lego

LEGO is the biggest toy company in the world with almost seven toy sets sold every second! That is approximately 600,000 sets sold a day. It has a market value of over $9 billion. This is a testament to the power of innovation whilst staying true to what they stand for. For over 80 years, Lego has been entertaining children and adults alike with its colourful, interlocking building blocks, and today the company is a global powerhouse in the toy industry.

LEGO innovated when they launched their 'LEGO Ideas' line which allows customers to submit their own ideas for Lego sets, giving them the chance to become part of the Lego family. The Lego Group allows users to submit ideas for Lego products to be turned into potential sets available commercially, with the original designer receiving 1% of the royalties. This is also a great example of the co-creation concept which we will cover in Chapter 8.

Lego's success can be traced back to its humble beginnings in 1932, when Danish carpenter Ole Kirk Christiansen began making wooden toys in his workshop. Two years later, he named his company LEGO after the Danish phrase leg godt ('play well'). Over the years, Christiansen expanded his business, and in 1949 he introduced the first Lego bricks, which were made from a plastic material called cellulose acetate, developed in the spirit of traditional wooden blocks that could be stacked upon one another but could be 'locked' together. These 'bricks' became an instant hit with children, and formed the foundation of what would become the Lego system of play. The Lego Group estimates that in five decades it has produced 400 billion Lego blocks. Annual production of Lego bricks averages approximately 36 billion, or about 1140 elements per second.

LEGO has always been innovative. Even in the 1950s and 1960s, LEGO started innovating with new themes such as the Town Plan and it developed new building techniques, such as the sliding brick, which allowed for greater creativity and imagination.

1961 and 1962 saw the introduction of the first Lego wheels, an addition that expanded the potential for building cars, trucks, buses, and other vehicles from Lego bricks. Also, during this time, the Lego Group introduced toys targeted explicitly at the pre-school market. In the late 1970s, the grandson of the founder and newly minted MBA, Kjeld Kirk Kristiansen, quickly unleashed a wave of innovation. He introduced the Technic brand in 1977 aimed at older kids, action sets with mini figures and more elaborate and ambitious models.

In the 1990s, growth slowed for several reasons, among which was the rise of brands such as Nintendo and Sony with their digital solutions. Toys "R" Us and other competitors began to take market share. This, combined with the expiry of the paten of the LEGO brick, led to the decline of LEGO. In 1999, LEGO refocused its innovation efforts on revolutionary toys that would change play forever.

In 1999, LEGO developed a new concept called 'Lego Mindstorms', a hardware and software structure which develops programmable robots based on Lego building blocks. Each version comes with computer Lego bricks, a set of modular sensors and motors, and parts from the Lego Technic line to create mechanical systems.

The system is controlled by the Lego bricks. It was unlike anything else on the market at the time, but it proved to be a huge success. The Mindstorms product helped Lego expand its reach and deepen its engagement with its customers.

In 2000, LEGO went on an innovation binge, adding LEGO-branded electronics, amusement parks, interactive video games, jewellery, education centres, and alliances with the Harry Potter franchise and Star Wars movies to its portfolio. At first, some of these initiatives worked, especially the Harry Potter and Star Wars product lines. However, these products were only successful in the years when a new movie or book was released. Other toys either failed to gain traction or were only popular within small niche markets. By 2003, the company was virtually out of cash. It lost $300 million that year, the projected loss for the next year was up to $400 million, and Lego was $800 million in debt.

What LEGO did next was important. They learnt.

- They Regained Focus
- They Found New Markets to Dominate
- They Got to Really Know Their Audience

Kirk Christiansen realised that he had to make a change to get LEGO back on track. He turned to a report from management consultant, Jorgen Vig Knudstorp. The report stated that LEGO needed to better organise and control its cutting-edge ambitions. Christiansen decided to step aside and let Knudstorp become CEO whilst he remained as Chairman.

The company sold a 70% stake in its successful Legoland theme parks for $460 million to the Blackstone Group and closed the firm's Danish office headquarters, moving management into a nearby factory. It then outsourced the overwhelming majority of its plastic brick production to cheaper facilities in Mexico and the Czech Republic. The new regime at LEGO, did not stop innovating. They created a more organised structure for the innovation process. Management gave everyone from the sales force to headquarters staff the opportunity to create and suggest new avenues for growth. But their ideas were put to the test: Any innovation had to prove to be consistent with the company goal of LEGO being recognised as the best company for family products.

LEGO continued to place emphasis on innovation but with a more structured approach. The company kept producing new and innovative products such as the Lego Digital Designer. LEGO Digital Designer (LDD) was a free software that was launched in 2004 that allowed users to build models with virtual LEGO bricks. At that point, LDD was a game changer as it made Lego accessible to a new generation of fans who were comfortable with digital technologies. LDD continued until 2016 as a simple building programme, at which point it stopped receiving funds for updates. A final update was available in 2019, and the programme has existed in limbo since. Since January 31, 2022, LDD has no longer been available for download.

LEGO's commitment to innovation is still going strong. As former CEO, Knudstorp, once said, ***'We need to constantly become better, or otherwise there will be someone out there who will catch up to us.'*** LEGO and Epic Games also announced they are entering a long-term partnership to shape the future of the metaverse to make it safe and fun for children and families. The two companies will team up to build an immersive, creatively inspiring and engaging digital experience for kids of all ages to enjoy.

The family-friendly digital experience will give kids access to tools that will empower them to become confident creators and deliver amazing play opportunities in a safe and positive space. It also recently launched a new web-based augmented reality (AR) experience to promote its new LEGO Technic Ferrari Daytona SP3 set which allows users and supercar fans to witness the Ferrari Daytona SP3's design and aerodynamics in augmented reality before purchasing the LEGO Technic set.

As Lego's story illustrates, if a brand wants to survive, its leaders must continually ask why. To truly understand what is working and what is not working, they have to constantly question the trajectory of a brand and continue experimenting. They need to realise that whilst the key to success is to continue to experiment and innovate, this has to be done in a controlled and structured manner with validated learnings and a clear objective. Unchecked innovation not aligned to the company's strategy and goals could be disastrous.

In 2003, Lego was $800 million in debt. Sales were down and the future was looking pretty bleak for the Danish toy company. Just over a decade later, in 2015, Lego had miraculously become the world's most powerful brand, boasting profits of $600 million.

In summary, when an organisation encourages the spirit experimentation and innovation, transformation is generally easier to execute, as it is already embedded in the company culture.

> **"An organization's ability to learn, and translate that learning into action rapidly, is the ultimate competitive advantage."**
>
> - Jack Welch, the former CEO of General Electric (GE)

> **"Innovation requires failure. If you're not failing, you're not innovating enough. It's okay to make mistakes. The important thing is to learn from them."**
>
> - Jørgen Vig Knudstorp, former CEO of the LEGO Group

If you would like to delve deeper into the concepts covered in this chapter, I recommend the following books:

Validated learning - The Lean Startup, by Eric Ries.

Experimentation and innovation - Think Like a Rocket Scientist, by Ozan Varol.

04

Technology

Next, let's look at technology and the part it plays in a business's transformation strategy.

When it comes to transformation, in particular, digital transformation, investing in the right technology is key. But before you start throwing money at the latest and greatest tech trends, it is important to have a vision and strategy in place. Technology is but a tool. It is what you do with it that counts. And, if you do not have a clear idea of where you are going and how you are going to get there, even the best technology in the world will not result in a successful digital transformation exercise. This is similar to starting a road trip with no plan or destination in mind - you may have a car that can get you there, but without a plan of where to go and how to get there, you may get lost or worst still, you may never reach your destination!

So, let us remember with the basics. What is digital transformation? Simply put, it is the integration of digital technology into all areas of a business, leading to fundamental changes to how the business operates and delivers value to customers.

With all the new and exciting technologies available in the market these days, it is very tempting to dive headfirst and invest in these latest technologies. However, it is extremely crucial to take a step back and consider the bigger picture. Having clear objectives and strategies is the first step. Asking and answering the questions below is a good starting point.

What are your business goals? Keep your customer in mind as a customer centric approach is key. What are the challenges and pain points that are currently stopping you from achieving these goals? What are the guiding principles that need to be established to overcome these challenges? What are the action plans needed to execute the guiding principles? What does success look like for your company in a digital world? Answering these questions will help you build a vision for your digital transformation and give you a roadmap for choosing the right technology.

When you have answered these questions as an organisation and have a clear vision, ensure that there is buy-in from top to bottom. Transformation is not a project that you can dabble in. You have to be committed to it. Once you have a clear vision that is aligned with stakeholders, it is time to start evaluating technology options. With so many choices out there, how do you choose the right one for your business?

The list below is not a comprehensive list but it includes important elements that should be considered.

First step is to review your current overall technology infrastructure. Does the system(s) in place have the capability to deliver what is needed from the transformation project? Can the existing system(s) be upgraded or integrated with new technologies? If these are possible solutions, then it can potentially help minimise cost and disruption to the business. But if not, then you might need to break out the chequebook and hope that the boss does not get a heart attack!

Next step is to think about the future needs of the business. It is impossible to know what the future holds with certainty, but it is worth investigating what is available in the market to fit the foreseeable needs of the business. It is also important to find a solution that is flexible and scalable so that it can adapt to any change in business requirement further down the road. Look into concepts such as unified commerce and composable commerce, especially if you are a B2C business.

Alignment is vital that when choosing the technology. Is it aligned to the business goals and objectives now and for the foreseeable future? For example, if the need is to better understand and improve customer experience, then the options are to either choose a basic CRM system or would it better to consider a marketing automation or a customer data platform that would provide predictive analytics and personalised content to the customers?

Cost is also a key element when choosing the right solution for the business. It is easy to get carried away and pick new and exciting technologies with all the bells and whistles but does the business need everything that the solution is offering? Are there modules that are not needed and might turn out to be a 'white elephant'? Also key is to ensure that the full cost is considered including license cost, professional services, implementation, training, maintenance, support, any potential integration cost and training.

Finally, it is extremely important to ensure that the right vendor is picked for the implementation. The solution can be from a big and reputable company but the partner implementing the solution is crucial. Consider the vendor's track record and their ability to support your business over the long term. Will they be around to provide updates and support as your needs change? Do they have a history of delivering reliable, secure, and scalable technology solutions? Get feedback from past implementation projects and past clients of the vendor.

Choosing a vendor to implement the solution is like choosing a life partner. You want someone reliable whom you can trust and who will stand by you in times of difficulty. You need to do your due diligence to research their experience, track record, and references to ensure that they are the right partner for the long-term. Get this wrong and you are in for a long and difficult journey that will cause you unnecessary stress and pain.

Now that we have covered the topic of how to choose the right technology for your digital transformation project, let us discuss some points on why investing in the right technology is so important.

The right technology provides your business with the agility and flexibility to accelerate and scale accordingly. The right technology is similar to having the right tools in a toolbox, allowing you to have everything you need to build something great. It provides your business with the means to tackle any challenge quickly and effectively.

More importantly, when a business invests in the right technology, it can play an important role in future proofing the business. In today's digital era, where it is very fast paced with a constantly evolving environment, the ability to be agile and adapt to new technologies and changing customer demands is essential for long term success (we will delve deeper into the concept of Lean & Agile in Chapter 7)

Investing in the right technology can also help a business in the following areas:

Improve Efficiency and Productivity - Technology can help make your employees and business more efficient and productive. Automation and Robotic Process Automation helps automate manual and repetitive processes which in return frees up valuable time and resources for more value-added tasks. These solutions can also reduce human error, thus improving accuracy and consistency in operations.

Improve Customer Experience – The right technology can help improve customer experience. An example is the use of Customer Data Platforms (CDP). It collects and unifies first-party customer data from multiple sources to build a single, coherent and complete view of each customer and then makes that data available to marketeers to create targeted and personalised marketing campaigns. This enables the business to personalise marketing messages and product recommendations for the customer, which helps create a more relevant experience when the customer interacts with the business. This ultimately leads to improved loyalty and repeat business.

Better Collaboration and Communication – Technology can also improve communication internally within an organisation. For example, team collaborative software such as Slack, employee engagement app such as KNOW and JUMBOW helps improve communication between employees making it a more efficient workplace. This can help to reduce confusion and increase accountability, leading to improved teamwork and overall performance.

Enhance Data Analysis and Data Management – Data is in abundance in today's world and a company needs to be able to ensure that it is using the data available in a productive manner. Companies that are not data driven will lose out to their competitors who are leveraging data. Data management technology has made organising data much easier. For instance, with a data catalogue software, businesses can easily keep track of all their data in one place. This allows companies to create a central database where all data files are stored. Predictive analytics hardware and software solutions can be utilised for discovery, evaluation and deployment of predictive scenarios by processing big data.

Competitive Advantage – To stay relevant in the industry that you are competing in, we have seen that the company has to experiment and innovate. This will allow the company to be adaptable to changes in the industry. Companies can differentiate themselves from their competitors and better meet the needs of their customers if they invest in technology.

Attract and retain top talent – Success of a business is down to its workforce. You can have the best strategy and technology but if the people in the business do not possess the right skill set and are the best at what they do, then your business is going to suffer. By providing digital tools and technologies that enhance the overall workplace experience, organisations can create a more engaging and fulfilling work environment for employees. It can also create new roles and career paths for employees, allowing them to develop new skills and advance their careers within the organisation. This will also help attract and retain talent for the company.

As a reminder, a digital transformation project is an ever evolving journey, not a destination. It is essentially a road map and not set in stone. There will be iterations and changes needed as the world around us changes. Being able to choose the right technology is crucial for a smooth journey. Having a clear vision, strategy, and objective together with carefully evaluating the options before choosing to invest in a particular technology will go a long way in ensuring that you have a successful digital transformation project and will set your business up for success in the future.

Unified Commerce and Composable Commerce

Unified Commerce refers to a business strategy that involves the integration of all sales channels, including social media, online, mobile, and in-store shopping. This approach aims at creating an uninterrupted customer experience where shoppers can interact with brands anywhere and anytime, they wish while enjoying consistency in terms of convenience, quality service delivery as well as personalised experiences. Unlike omnichannel retail which operates each channel separately with different inventories and pricing strategies, unified commerce utilises a centralised platform for real-time inventory management alongside customer profiling for optimal pricing optimisation.

For example, retailers can improve their ability to cater to customers' requirements promptly and with greater precision by adopting unified commerce. In addition, they can provide customised suggestions and offers while monitoring customer conduct across multiple channels for a better understanding of their buying habits and preferences. By adopting this approach, retailers stand to enhance consumer contentment as well as brand loyalty, optimise supply chain efficiency while cutting down operational expenses in the midst of intense competition, especially within the retail industry.

Composable commerce is a contemporary method of constructing an architecture that enables businesses to create a flexible and adaptable commerce platform by integrating various top-notch commerce services and features. This concept is rooted in the notion of composable architecture, which entails dividing intricate systems into smaller modular components that can be effortlessly combined or replaced without completely revamping the entire system.

With composable commerce, companies can take advantage of pre-designed third-party commerce services like payment processing, shipping options, fraud detection methods and tax calculation tools, merging them seamlessly with their own commerce platform. By taking this approach, organisations can handpick the most suitable functionalities and services for their specific requirements while being able to switch out for better alternatives whenever necessary.

Businesses that require flexibility in adapting to market changes, customer needs and technological advancements find the composable commerce model appealing. Through this approach, businesses can establish a resilient and cost-effective infrastructure capable of accommodating growth and innovation. Composable commerce further enables companies to streamline time-to-market processes while improving their operational efficiency and enhancing overall customer experience.

Walmart

Walmart's transformation story is a great example of a successful digital transformation journey. Walmart started out with humble beginnings as a small discount store in Arkansas and has grown to what it is today– a global retail giant. As a business, Walmart has undergone significant transformation with a digital-first approach at the centre of its transformation. Let us go through some of Walmart's history and how it managed to transform successfully.

On July 2, 1962, Sam Walton opened the first Walmart store in Rogers, Arkansas. By 1969, the company was officially incorporated and registered $12.7 billion in sales. Walmart actually launched without a true logo. In fact, for the first two years, when the Walmart name appeared in print, the font and style were chosen at the whim of the printer. In 1964, Walmart selected a logo font. This 'Frontier Font Logo' was the first official and first consistently used logo in Walmart's history. By 1990, Walmart was the number one retailer in the U.S. As the Walmart Supercenter redefined convenience and one-stop shopping, Everyday Low Prices went global. In 1997, Walmart celebrated a year that brought in $100 billion in sales eventually becoming the largest retailer in the world.

In the early 2000's Walmart, like many other physical retail companies, faced new challenges. The rise of e-commerce brands such as Amazon and the increased convenience of shopping online was a big threat to the traditional retail model. Walmart responded by implementing a digital first strategy which began with the launch of its very own e-commerce channel in 2000. While Walmart's early digital efforts were focused mainly on selling goods online, the company soon realised that they needed to do more to keep up with the rapidly changing retail landscape.

In 2011, Walmart acquired social media startup Kosmix, which later became @WalmartLabs, the company's technology innovation arm. @WalmartLabs was tasked with finding new and innovative ways to use technology to enhance the Walmart shopping experience, both in-store and online. One of the key initiatives to come out of @WalmartLabs was the launch of Walmart's first mobile app, which allowed customers to easily shop, compare prices, and check out with just a few taps. Jet.com was acquired in August 2016, when Walmart got serious about selling online. Jet.com founder, Marc Lore, then became the CEO of Walmart's U.S. e-commerce operations and has since been driving Walmart's digital revolution.

Walmart also launched their online grocery service which involves a combination of online and offline interactions between the customer and the retailer. Customers shop online via the Walmart website, adding items to their cart which they can even save throughout the week as they build their order if they choose. They have an option of either having the groceries delivered to their homes or pick it up at the store or kerbside pick-up. The launch of the online grocery service was a huge success and helped Walmart establish itself as a leader in the e-commerce space.

What made Walmart's digital transformation so successful? The linchpins of Walmart's transformation are digital innovation, products, focus on customers and its people.

Customer focused – Walmart has always focused on providing the best possible shopping experience for its customers. Instead of charging too much for products, Walmart maximises its income by making prices customer-friendly and focusing on bulk sales. Walmart is known for its superior procurement methods in negotiating prices to keep costs low. Walmart is also constantly looking for ways to use make shopping easier, faster, and more convenient for its customers by leveraging on technology.

Investment in technology – Walmart focused on digitalising almost all areas of its business, from the supply chain to sales, customer service, marketing, and store operations. Investment in technology was also a key strategy for Walmart. They invested in two ways: investing and acquiring startups that were disrupting the industry (from brands like Moosejaw and Bonobos to the largest online retailer in India, Flipkart) and investing in its own innovation lab, @WalmartLabs. These initiatives allowed Walmart to be at the forefront of new technological advancements in the retail space.

Integration of technology and brick-and-mortar stores – Walmart has been successful in its digital transformation because it has leveraged technology to enhance its brick-and-mortar stores, rather than trying to replace them. For example, the company's online grocery service is integrated with its physical stores, allowing customers to pick up their groceries in-store or have them delivered to their homes.

Experimentation, Innovation and Agility – Walmart embraced the concepts of experimentation, innovation and agility. This culture ensures the success that Walmart sees today. From trying new things, like the launch of its online grocery service to being quick to pivot and making changes when necessary.

People – Walmart's people working behind and alongside its digital platforms are the real secret weapon that will continue to power its transformation into a technology company. Investing in growth starting with on the job which Walmart feels is the best form of growth and development.

Hiring somebody frontline and giving them a mobile device that includes job prompts and information about their employment and enables them to build connections is super important. We have an app that allows people to be successful on the job," stated Walmart's Chief People Officer Donna Morris.

Walmart also established Walmart Academy, which provides a foundation of not just virtual learning and development but also brick-and-mortar development. They also have a great university and secondary education programme called Live Better U, with more than 75,000 associates engaged in the programme as at the end of 2022.

Walmart also gets all of their top leaders to think about being the Chief Customer Officer. Walmart believes that if the leaders all have the lens of being a Chief Customer Officer, they will then do more to unlock the potential for the business.

Walmart's digital transformation strategy has been a hugely successful. They have embraced the culture of continuing improvement and innovation which has helped the company to remain relevant in an ever-evolving landscape and has established itself as one of the leaders in the retail space. The focus on customer experience, investing in technology, integrating technology and brick-and-mortar stores, and being agile and willing to experiment, have allowed Walmart to create a shopping experience that is seamless and convenient.

"We're going to make shopping with us faster, easier and more enjoyable. We'll do more than just save customers money and you, our associates, will make the difference. Looking ahead, we will compete with technology, but win with people. We will be people-led and tech-empowered."

- Walmart CEO, Doug McMillon

Contribution by Agata Bas, Customer Growth and Digital Experiences Expert

One cannot talk about digital transformation without putting customer experience at its heart. Like any buzzword, it is broad and often misinterpreted. To understand how digital transformation impacts the way your customers interact with your brand, we must take a closer look at consumer evolution.

Covid has accelerated digital adoption, meaning many consumers who were slow to adapt to discovering and buying online are now regular e-commerce visitors. Everyone has realised the convenience of shopping online, and they are not going back to their past habits, or at least not in the same form. Instead of planning a shopping trip to the mall, they are always shopping online. According to Thinkwithgoogle, 84% of Americans are shopping for something at any given time and in up to six different categories. Instead of traveling to the other side of the city to pick up an item, they have it delivered to their doorstep. Instead of calling customer support, they prefer to read reviews and use instant chat. And finally, instead of sticking to one brand forever, they keep exploring and are open to trying new things.

According to McKisney in their post Covid consumer trends, '75 percent of consumers tried new shopping behaviours, with many of them citing convenience and value. Fully 39 percent of them, mainly Gen Z and millennials, deserted trusted brands for new ones.'

Today's customer is not one dimensional. They still appreciate the offline experience and take the best of both worlds in an unplanned manner. They might research online, want to try it in a physical shop, but then order the item to be delivered to their homes. And, they demand that every touchpoint recognises them and that the entire journey is seamless, intuitive, and delightful. The modern consumer is picky, and because digitalisation has lowered the barriers to entry for brands in virtually any space. They know that there will be another brand that can fulfil their needs better in the occurrence of an unsatisfying experience with one brand.

What does this mean for brands? You need to be where your customers are, when they need you, and how they want to interact with your brand. This is just the bare minimum. The competitive market requires companies that want to sustainably grow to take the extra step by providing a memorable and referral-worthy experience. This is where digital transformation is not the end goal but a means to deliver your brand promise.

There are a few good examples of companies that have delivered their brand promise via digital transformation that I would like to highlight. Starting with Starbucks, which is an inspiration for business digitalisation and forward thinking for most retail players. The brand promises a consistent experience and connection to inspire and nurture the human spirit. 25 years ago, Starbucks's focus was mainly on in-store experience, but with the rise of online channels, the company realised that the customer experience starts way before entering the store and that the customer journey became way more complex.

They knew early on that digital channels would be the key to maintaining delivery of their mission. Starbucks embarked on their digital journey in 2009, launching the Starbucks Card Mobile with MyStarbucks app followed by their loyalty program and mobile payments. Starbucks was one of the first in retail to introduce digital wallet successfully, giving the brand the longstanding title of the most popular mobile payment in the USA. Only a few years ago, it was overtaken by Apple Pay, which allows payments across all industries and not just one store like Starbucks.

Starbucks has successfully leveraged data and AI to provide a highly personalised online-to-offline experience, and their loyalty program has over 16 million active members (as of January 2023), making it one of the most successful loyalty programs in the world. The solid foundation and data collection allowed Starbucks to leverage drive-through options during COVID-19 lockdowns, and the brand's agility enabled fast decisions to open more convenient pick-up stores for customers. Starbucks also uses the latest technology and innovation to improve processes, supply, and operational efficiency to provide the best experience possible. Starbucks, recognised for over two decades as the world's most admired company by Fortune, is a great example of leading the change and embodying innovation that, as a result, serves customers better than yesterday.

The other worth-mentioning example is Ikea, the famous furniture retail store known for their iconic printed catalogues sent to clients' mailboxes back in the day. Their mission is to create a better everyday life for the many people, and they go beyond just affordable and functional furnishing. A couple of years before the pandemic, they embraced digital transformation and took the challenge of retaining the value and brand promise while transitioning to the new digital reality, under the condition of creating human-centric technology.

Since then, they have acquired over 20 companies to support their strategy and fulfill the long-term goal. Ikea was one of the first retailers to launch WebGL and AR technology to allow customers to virtually place furniture in their own space in true-to-scale 3D in real-time, which quickly gained popularity among customers and enabled personalisation at scale for Ikea. But the broader digital transformation, due to the complexity of their model and legacy of an analogue business, was a long process, accelerated rapidly only with the occurrence of the pandemic. As a symbol of their commitment to the new digital reality, they ended the 70-year-old tradition of printed catalogues.

They then shifted their stores into fulfillment facilities to support 24/7 e-commerce that will improve delivery speed for consumers and efficiency for the company. In 2021, the company reported that "IKEA online channels welcomed more than 5 billion visitors this year, and online retail sales increased 73%."

The brand realises that as important as digital channels are, customers still like visiting physical shops and human connections. While investing in digital channels, they simultaneously grow their brick-and-mortar stores, innovating on various formats, locations, and sizes. The experience needs to be further elevated. In some countries, they introduced the "Shop and Go" feature for customers to scan and pay for items using their mobile phones to avoid checkout queues, a great example of using technology to solve the pinpoint that often negatively influences customer experience. They are also improving online and offline experience with a growing number of digital in-store kiosks and meeting points with IKEA staff. Ikea is an astonishing example for 'changing everything but the brand's DNA' and undergoing complex transformation putting people and consumer in the heart of the process.

Lastly, the example of Nike, which does not just sell shoes and sports attire like its competitors. Nike lives and breathes the mission of inspiring and empowering people to embrace an athletic lifestyle. Since 2020, its strategy is heavily concentrated on digital and data collection. To stay ahead of the competition and to be always desired by customers, Nike focuses on selling directly to consumers by building complex data capabilities in-house to be always agile, responsive to market opportunities, and more importantly, build a deep, direct relationship with their customers.

As their brand promise is to inspire, they offer various digitally empowered initiatives to cater to all types of consumers and their motivation triggers. For those who get stimulus from community and accountability, they offer popular app memberships like Nike Run Club and Nike Training Club. For the new generation of future loyal customers, they hopped early on into the metaverse and NFT. For those who appreciate exclusivity, they offer Nike By You, which allows users to design their shoes, and finally, for those who are just starting their sporting adventures, they provide an AR tool that allows accurate measurement of foot size and match it with optimal shoes.

Thanks to their commitment to innovation powered by integrated data, the experience is seamless and exciting for all. Nike, the most valuable apparel brand in the world, is an example of a true innovative mindset that understands the new digital reality and meets customers where they will be tomorrow, executing their digital transformation strategy spotlessly.

Digital transformation is an unavoidable progression for any player in the market. As many companies build agile, customer-centric cultures, and with the rise of new players that are digital natives and unburdened by legacy systems and processes, they have an advantage in catering to the new consumer, leaving behind companies that are resistant to thinking progressively.

However, the key to undergoing adjustments to this new reality is to understand your customers better than ever before and stay true to your brand promise, implementing technology that enables its delivery in an ever-evolving way.

Sources:

https://www.mckinsey.com/capabilities/growth-marketing-and-sales/our-insights/emerging-consumer-trends-in-a-post-covid-19-world
https://hbr.org/2021/03/10-truths-about-marketing-after-the-pandemic
https://www.thinkwithgoogle.com/consumer-insights/consumer-trends/shopping-occasion-experiences/
https://www.forrester.com/blogs/order-up-starbucks-rewards-changes-signal-a-renewed-focus-on-profitable-loyalty/
https://d3.harvard.edu/platform-digit/submission/starbucks-leveraging-big-data-and-artificial-intelligence-to-improve-experience-and-performance/
https://one.starbucks.com/get-the-facts/starbucks-named-worlds-most-admired/ https://www.insiderintelligence.com/content/apple-pay-overtakes-starbucks-as-top-mobile-payment-app-in-the-us
https://www.thinkwithgoogle.com/intl/en-154/future-of-marketing/digital-transformation/ikea-omnichannel-engagement/amp/

05

Platform As A Business Model

One of the concepts that businesses should consider leveraging is the Platform as a business model. Whilst many may feel that this mainly applies to the retail industry, such as a marketplace, this is far from the truth. Irrespective of the industry that you are in, considering how this concept can be used to help your business could be very beneficial.

It may be that it will not be suitable for your business, but I recommend understanding the concept and experimenting on how it could be integrated as part of your business.

Let us start by understanding the concept.

Platform vs Pipeline

The traditional business model is called 'Pipeline' business model. It is essentially how a business designs, creates a product, markets it and sells to the customer. Pipeline businesses use the Porter's value chain model. Porter described a chain of activities common to all businesses, and he divided them into primary and support activities, as shown in the illustration below.

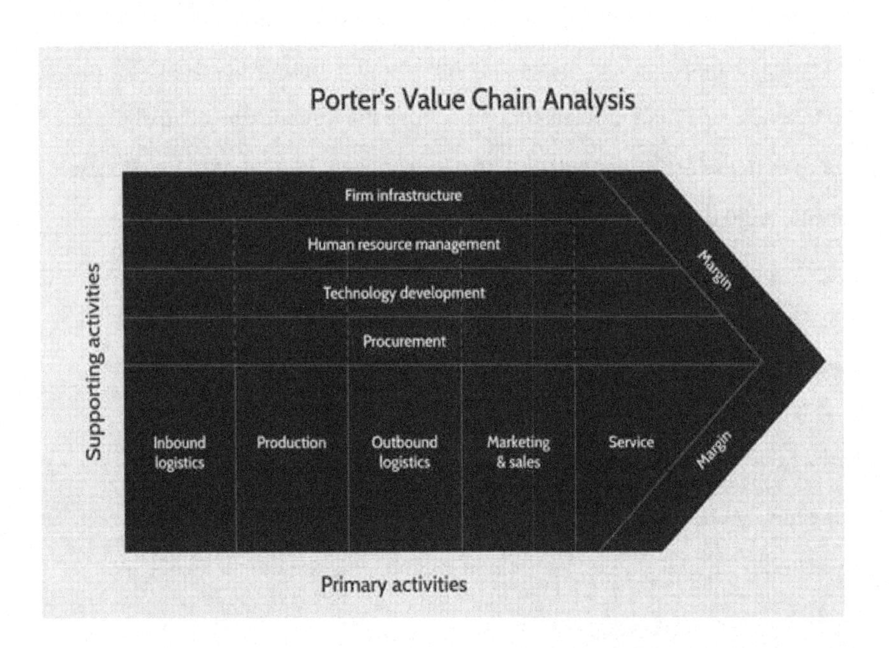

In the current digital world, businesses are increasingly shifting from the pipeline business model to the platform business model, which is made up of producers and consumers, some of whom play both roles of producer and consumer.

The concept of 'Platform as a business model' sounds like a simple concept but it has been disrupting the traditional business model in recent years. It has become popular with the growth in the power of the internet and digital technologies. It is a business model that uses technology to connect people, organisations, and resources in an interactive ecosystem where huge value can be created and exchanged by using network effects. Network effects is a key advantage of this business model. (We will cover the network effect separately in the next section.) Platform businesses are taking over every industry and are already a part of our everyday lives whether we realise it or not. Airbnb, Uber, Alibaba, Facebook, Upwork and Instagram are all examples of successful companies that harnessed the power of the platform.

Platform businesses are not a new concept. Think about physical marketplaces or malls, department stores, or even exhibition centres. These business models mostly relied on brick-and-mortar infrastructure to enable interactions and exchange values. Advancement in technology has shifted this business mode online and helps scale participation and collaboration. It is similar to how the invention of the internet changed the way people communicate with one another by allowing them to connect much easier and faster than before. The advancement of technology has helped businesses to do the same, connecting sellers and buyers from around the world and allowing them to transact easier and faster.

What is a 'Platform'? One of the best definitions I have come across is from the book. Platform Revolution by Geoffrey G. Parker, Marshall W. Van Alstyne and Sangeet Paul Chaoudary. They defined it as:

'A business based on enabling value-creating interactions between external producers and consumers. The platform provides an open, participative infrastructure for these interactions and sets governance conditions for them. The Platform's overarching purpose is to consummate matches among users and facilitate the exchange of goods, services or social currency, thereby enabling value creation for all participants.'

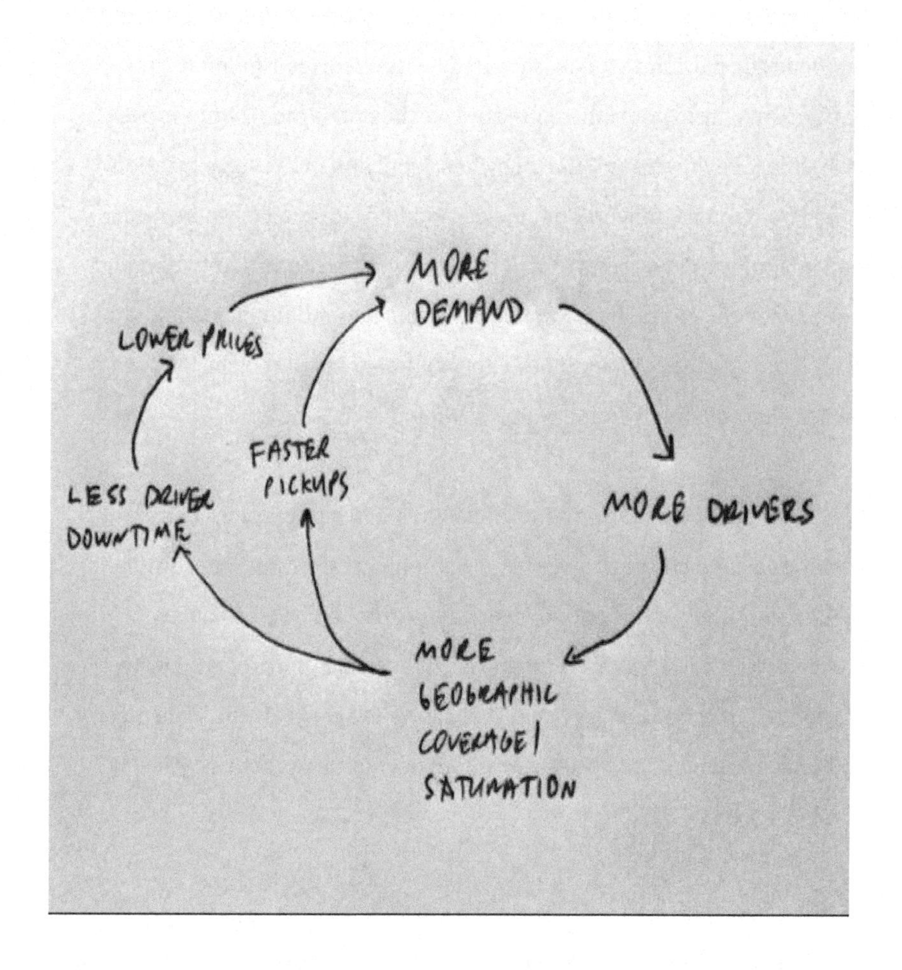

David Sack's napkin sketch of Uber's chain of events is a great example of the platform business model.

One of the important elements of this business model is that a significant portion of the platform's value is created by its users (community). The platform business model therefore shifts its business model from focusing on internal activities to external activities. More and more, value creation comes from outside the firm not inside, and from external partners rather than internal employees. As functions ranging from marketing to operations are increasingly being shifted to people, resources, and functions that are located outside the business, they either complement or replace those that have been traditionally found within a traditional business.

An advantage of the platform model is that it can scale rapidly as it leverages assets and resources of the community of users. For example, in the case of Airbnb, it does not own any of the properties listed on its platform. Instead, it leverages the assets of its users (the property owners) to provide accommodation services. This allows the company to scale quickly and offer a wide range of services without having to invest heavily in physical assets.

For traditional business models, during the industrial era especially, businesses grew and took significant portions of market share based on the concept of supply economies of scale. This concept revolves around values such as production efficiencies, reducing the unit cost of a product as the quantity being produced increases.

We can see this in real life manufacturing examples where the term 'MOQ' is used, which refers to Minimum Order Quantity and typically, the cost per unit is the highest at the MOQ level and reduces when more units are produced in that particular manufacturing run. The supply economies of scale gave the largest companies a cost advantage that it becomes almost impossible for competitors to overcome.

In today's world, this is changing. There are still industrial players benefiting from supply economies of scale but new players in the market are now taking significant market share by leveraging demand economies of scale. Consumers and their demand for goods and services are the key economic drivers when looking at demand economies of scale. This is driven by efficiencies in social networks, demand aggregation, app development, and other phenomena that make bigger networks more valuable to their users.

Demand side economies of scale exists in industries where the value of a product or service increases in accordance with the number of users of that product or service. Hence, the more users there are, the more valuable the product or service becomes.

It can give the largest company in a platform market a network effect advantage that is extremely difficult for competitors to overcome. This is now quickly becoming the main driver of economic value in today's digital world. This is not to say that supply economies of scale no longer matter; of course, they do. But demand economies of scale, in the form of network effects, has become the most important differentiating factor.

Network Effects

Let's understand what network effect is. There are 3 generally accepted laws that governs the spread of technology:

Moore's Law (Gordon Moore) – which states computing world dramatically increase in power with decrease in relative cost as an exponential rate.

Metcalfe's Law (Robert Metcalfe) – originator of Ethernet and founder of 3COM, stated the value of a telecommunications network is proportional to the square of the number of connected users of the system.

Bandwidth Law (George Gilder) – prolific author and prophet of the new technology age - the total bandwidth of communication systems triples every twelve months, as in bandwidth speed grows at least 3 times faster than computing power.

Metcalfe's law is a great example of explaining how network effects work and how they create value for those participating in that network. Robert Metcalfe pointed out that the value of a telephone network grows nonlinearly as the number of subscribers to the network increases., enabling more connections among subscribers. Basically, it illustrates that with just one phone in the world, it is practically of no value but as more people start using telephones, the value grows. Network effect can be observed in a variety of contexts, including online platforms, social networks, and communication technologies.

Network effects are evident in online platforms and social networks. As more people use them, these platforms become more valuable since they connect people, share information, and provide them with a wide range of services. Online platforms and social networks have a network effect that has made them such powerful tools for communication and commerce, and also made them extremely valuable companies. Instagram and Facebook are great examples, where they became more useful and thus more valuable as more and more people joined.

Network effect can also be easily seen taking effect in online communication tools such instant messaging platforms, email, and text messaging. When increasingly more users on-board these platforms, the more valuable the platform becomes, as they allow people to communicate with each other quickly and easily, regardless of where they are located. Network effect apparent in these platforms have revolutionise how people communicate.

Innovation and competition can also be affected by the network effect. By capturing a large and growing user base, companies that can create and harness the network effect can dominate their respective markets. Due to this, new entrants often struggle to compete because they can't match the established players' network effect. Network effect also encourages businesses to keep innovating which results in companies creating new and better products and services.

All these examples are usually called positive network effects.

It is also good to understand that there is also such a thing as negative network effect. The growth of a network can also potentially produce negative network effects that could drive away participants. In a negative network effect as the network grows in usage or scale, the value of the platform might shrink. In platform business models network effects help the platform become more valuable for the next user joining. Negative network effects (congestion or pollution) reduce the value of the platform for the next user joining.

Examples of negative network effect:

Reduced quality of matching – when there are increasing consumers and producers on the platform, there is a possibility that the quality of matches reduces, which makes the platform less valuable or frustrating to the user. The Platform needs to ensure that it keeps the curation level high so that the quality of the platform is not compromised.

Network congestion – whereby too many users can slow a network down, reducing its utility and frustrating network members

To summarise, network effect is a phenomenon in which a product or service becomes more valuable as more people use it. This is because the value of the product or service increases as the number of users increases, creating a self-reinforcing cycle of adoption. By helping products gain traction quickly, network effects can help companies build formidable business moats — or strong competitive advantages that set them apart.

Platform Challenges

Whilst the platform business model offers numerous benefits and has become an increasingly popular business strategy, with many successful companies like Amazon, Uber, and Airbnb serving as examples of its potential, it has its fair share of challenges.

One of the challenges faced by many platform businesses is trust. For a platform to be successful, participants need to trust the concept behind the platform, the platform itself, and one another to make transactions. The nature of a platform will determine the nature of the level of trust stakeholders need because some activities require a greater level of confidence than others.

Fostering trust between platform participants is often the most important aspect when helping all participants trust the platform itself. For instance, eBay uses a feedback system and user ratings to build trust between buyers and sellers, while Airbnb uses user profiles, reviews, and ID checks. Another example is the difference between AirBnB and Craigslist. There is a higher level of trust with AirBnB compared to Craigslist, who has earned relatively low scores on the trust metric. AirBnB achieved this because of its ability to curate its participants successfully.

Trust is also strongly linked to the concept of matching in a platform business. The quality of matching must be of a very high level for a platform business. This refers to the accuracy of the search algorithm and the intuitiveness if the navigation tools offered to users as they seek other users with whom they can engage in value creating interactions. Therefore, if the platform is able to do a great job in linking users to one another (e.g. consumers and producers) quickly and accurately, users are far more likely to keep using the platform as opposed to a low quality and slow matching algorithm.

This usually ends up in the participants abandoning the platform relatively quickly. For example, if a website were to link a customer to a restaurant that was not what they were looking for, they would be far less likely to use it in the future. Technology changes can also be a challenge for a platform business. As new technologies emerge, such as AI and 5G, the platforms have to quickly identify how to leverage these technologies and improve the platform or offer more value-added service or it will be at risk of being outdated.

Competition is also another challenge for the platform business model. As the platform business model is highly scalable, making it easier for new entrants to enter the market, it can lead to increased competition and pressure on margins. For example, when Uber entered the market, it quickly gained market share and caused taxi companies to reduce their fares to compete, leading to a decrease in their profits. In Southeast Asia, Uber faced a competitor called Grab, who provided customers with promotion codes which could be used to obtain lower fares compared to Uber – to gain market share from Uber. Uber lost that battle and eventually sold its Southeast Asia business to Grab. Grab is now facing competition from Gojek in Southeast Asia.

Another important aspect of the platform business model is the pricing strategy. There are several ways that platform companies can generate revenue, including transaction fees, advertising, and subscription fees. The chosen pricing strategy will depend on the type of platform and the target market. For example, platforms serving businesses may choose to charge transaction fees, while consumer-focused platforms may opt for advertising or subscription fees. Pricing and monetisation of a platform business is one of the most difficult issues that any platform business must pay close attention to.

In summary, the platform business model is rapidly becoming an important business mode due to its advantages such as network effect and the ability to leverage user assets and resources, which allows it to grow and scale faster. According to UNCTAD[1] (2019), the total market value of platform companies with $100 million in market capital was roughly more than $7 trillion in 2017— 67% higher than in 2015. However, as we have seen, there are also challenges, including trust, competition issues and the need to carefully consider pricing strategy.

According to a research report by McKinsey, digital platforms could mediate around $60 trillion of global economic activity within six years. However, experts believe that only 3% of existing companies have implemented a successful platform strategy.

1) UNCTAD - The United Nations Conference on Trade and Development is an intergovernmental organisation within the United Nations Secretariat that promotes the interests of developing countries in world trade.

AirBnB

It is well known that Airbnb has been one of the biggest success stories in the history of technology, and how it has leveraged the power of platform as a business model and the network effect to become a massive company. From the idea of a simple home-sharing platform, Airbnb was able to rapidly scale and expand to new markets, leveraging its platform to create a network of millions of users and hosts, and generating a significant economic impact for businesses and individuals alike. Let us see how AirBnB embraced some of the key concepts discussed earlier and grew its business to what it is today.

To recap, the platform business model is one where a company creates a platform that allows multiple parties to interact and transact with one another. AirBnB which provides a platform for people to list their properties for rent and for travellers to find a place to stay, is a great example to illustrate the business model.

Network effect - In the case of Airbnb, as more people listed their properties and more travellers used the platform to find a place to stay, the value of the platform increased. This in turn, attracted even more users, creating a self-reinforcing cycle of growth and adoption.

How did Airbnb get its start by taking advantage of the network effect to become a success? Well, the story starts with Craigslist. Back in 2007, co-founders Brian Chesky and Joe Gebbia had a problem: they needed to pay their rent, and they were short on cash. The pair knew a big design conference was coming to San Francisco, and it was making hotels hard to come by. So, they came up with an idea to rent out air mattresses in their living room and host attendees of the design conference. They created a simple site, airbedandbreakfast.com, bought three air mattresses, and arranged them in their loft.

This is where the platform as a business model comes in. They realised that there was a huge opportunity to connect people with extra space with travellers who needed a place to stay. So, they built a website called Airbnb and started listing their own space. They also leveraged the network effect by reaching out to friends and encouraging them to list their own properties on the platform.

It was not an instant success. In fact, they struggled early in the business and things did not go according to plan. They struggled to get traction and gain users. They continued to work on the platform, making improvements, adding new features, and making it more user-friendly. The company launched a second time, but no one noticed. The third time was at SXSW in 2008, but they only had two customers, and Chesky was one of them.

One of their key strategies for growth was to utilise the network effect of Craigslist. They realised that many people were already using Craigslist to look for a place to stay, so they decided to reach out to those users and encourage them to try Airbnb instead of investing in paid ads, or social media. Every time someone posted on Craigslist that they were offering their home up for a bed and breakfast or for short term lodging, they emailed them asking them if they wanted to list on their platform instead. This was manual as well as tedious, but it worked and was a low cost. They also offered discount to users who signed up for Airbnb after finding a listing on Craigslist. This helped to get the ball rolling and allowed Airbnb to tap into the existing network of users on Craigslist.

From there, things started to take off. The network effect kicked in, as more and more people started using Airbnb, more and more properties were listed on the platform. As the network grew, the value of the platform increased, which in turn attracted even more users. Airbnb also launched photography services to make offerings more appealing to guests and an added ability for mutual social connections to see who else had stayed at the property to build trust in the marketplace.

Today, Airbnb is a massive company with millions of users and listings in hundreds of cities around the world. It is an immense example of how a platform as a business model and the network effect can help to create a successful and valuable company.

If you would like to have a deeper understanding of the Platform as a Business Model concept, I recommend reading the following book:

Platform Revolution, by Geoffrey G. Parker, Marshall W. Van Alstyne and Sangeet Paul Chaoudary

> **'We used to live in a world where there are people, private citizens, a world where there are businesses, and now we're living in a world where people can become businesses in 60 seconds.'**
>
> - Brian Chesky, CEO, AirBnB

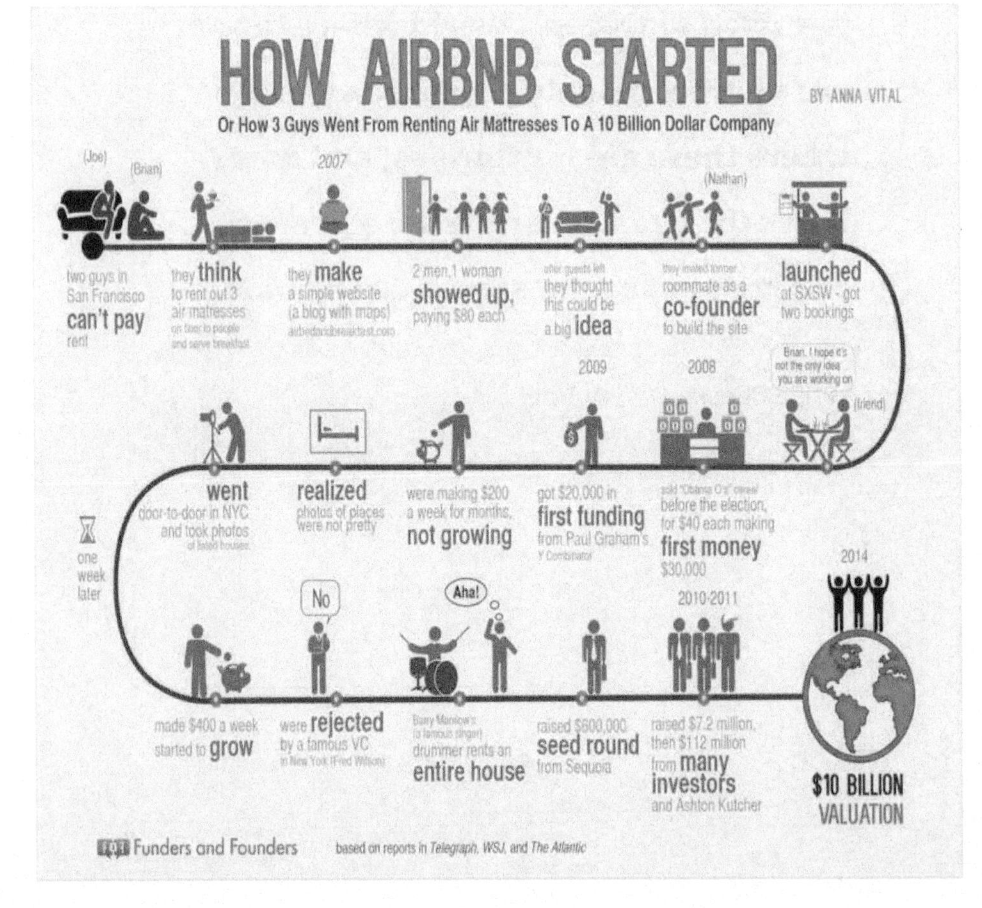
HOW AIRBNB STARTED
BY ANNA VITAL
Or How 3 Guys Went From Renting Air Mattresses To A 10 Billion Dollar Company
(Joe)
(Brian)
2007
(Nathan)
two guys in San Francisco can't pay rent
they think to rent out 3 air mattresses
they make a simple website (a blog with maps)
2 men,1 woman showed up, paying $80 each
they thought this could be a big idea
roommate as a co-founder to build the site
launched at SXSW - got two bookings
2009
2008
(friend)
went door-to-door in NYC and took photos
realized photos of places were not pretty
were making $200 a week for months, not growing
got $20,000 in first funding from Paul Graham's
before the election, for $40 each making first money $30,000
one week later
2014
2010-2011
No
Aha!
made $400 a week started to grow
were rejected by a famous VC
drummer rents an entire house
raised $600,000 seed round from Sequoia
raised $7.2 million, then $112 million from many investors and Ashton Kutcher
$10 BILLION VALUATION
Funders and Founders
based on reports in Telegraph, WSJ, and The Atlantic

06

People at the Centre of Transformation

The current digital era has brought many changes to the way we live and work. Businesses have realised that they are facing a new reality as they strive to keep up with the rapid pace of technological changes. Many understand the need to transform but are still unsure of how to go about transforming their business or how to start the transformation process. The recent pandemic has accelerated the need to transform and unfortunately, many companies jumped on the bandwagon without having a proper strategy in place.

A recent study by McKinsey revealed that 70% of all digital transformation projects end in failure. There are many reasons why a transformation project can result in failure but often, it is because of People. Many organisations tend to ignore or not prioritise its people when devising a digital transformation strategy and execution plan. As you have seen in the previous chapters, there is more to digital transformation than just embracing technology. It redefines the way the business operates, introduces new processes and new business models. These strategies, plans and execution are all carried out by people. Therefore, organisations that focus on transforming its people and culture at the start of their digital transformation projects are more likely to see success. For instance, companies such as Amazon and Netflix invested heavily in their people and culture to ensure they are ready to embrace digital transformation and its associated benefits. Having a People strategy is vital for a successful transformation project.

As we have now identified that People are crucial to the success of a digital transformation project, let us understand how companies establish a great People Strategy. Whilst understanding that a People Strategy is important, it is also equally important to understand what it is not. And, more specifically, how it differs from another type of business strategy you may be familiar with, such as HR (Human Resources) strategy. As far as HR and People strategies are concerned, there are definitely overlaps. Both strategies are led by human resource leaders and are both intended to provide employees with a better working environment.

Let us first understand the difference between the two strategies.

People Strategy versus HR Strategy

People strategy is all about talent management. In other words, managing human capital. It is about creating a positive environment for employees and helping them grow professionally and personally. One of the hardest parts about people strategy is supporting people now while also staying focused on the types of behaviours, skills, and capabilities that are needed in the future. It is an approach an organisation takes to build and develop its team in order to meet company goals.

HR strategy, on the other hand, is more about logistics. It focuses on creating a plan to manage the more logistical side of human resources management that is used to support the organisation's People strategy. HR strategy includes things like on-boarding, employee benefits, compensation, performance management, and training and development. In other words, HR strategy is the 'how' to the People strategy's 'what'.

It is important to distinguish between People and HR strategies as understanding what each strategy entails, helps the organisation define and execute the strategies better. If an organisation only focuses on HR strategy, it might miss out on important opportunities for attracting, retaining, and developing the right people. If an organisation only focuses on people strategy, it might miss out on important opportunities for improving organisational performance.

Some examples of the two strategies:

HR strategy – Creating processes which include sourcing, payroll, interviewing, or PTO (paid time off), creating org charts, creating compensation plans, managing employee files and managing compliance.

People strategy – Creating employee growth and development plans, diversity hiring initiatives, fostering better cross-functional communication, driving and shaping company culture, collecting employee feedback and using that feedback to improve workplace experience, planning team events to foster belonging and inclusion.

Having the right people strategy and ensuring that this is given priority is at the crux of a successful digital transformation plan. It will create a culture that will help deliver the transformation plan, and this is important as a company's culture affects the decisions and actions of its employees at every level. As such, a company's culture will either serve as a major enabler or a major impediment to innovation or transformation, depending on how the company's culture is framed. This is especially true when it comes to digital transformation. That does not mean ignoring the HR strategy. The HR strategy plays an important role in supporting the People strategy.

Leadership

As we now know, for a business to stay competitive, it is fundamental that it embraces digital transformation. A company's culture is key to driving this digital transformation which entails new ways of thinking and new ways to collaborate. This must start from the very top.

Leaders of organisations need to be fully committed to building the right culture for the company. They also need to ensure that they themselves evolve and are adept to lead in this digital era. It is like a ship setting sail on a voyage; the captain needs to know how to navigate the waters, how to motivate the crew, and ensure that all are on the same path in order to reach their destination. Without the captain's leadership and commitment, the journey will be doomed to fail.

We have seen in previous chapters that the constant introduction of new technology, experimentation and innovation plays an important role in digital transformation. It is therefore crucial to ensure that there are capabilities within the organisation to select the right technology, and to integrate and implement them as part of the business strategy. Developing a Digital Age Leadership Capability is key to a successful digital transformation.

What are Digital Age capabilities and skill sets that leaders should have to succeed in this digital era?

There should be a shift in mindset to start. 'Mindset' – a set of beliefs and resulting attitudes that frame both our interpretation of situations we encounter, and our response to those situations. The beliefs that shape our mindset are deeply held positions based on our knowledge, experiences, environment, and culture. Our beliefs create an attitude regarding our willingness and ability to address each situation we encounter and strongly influence if, how, and how well we will act. A Mindset Shift is a change in beliefs and attitudes made in response to changes in one's environment.

An explanation of this was illustrated in the Blockbuster example earlier on in the book. Blockbuster's leadership team did not shift their mindset to align with changes in their environment. Instead, they kept the mindset that had enabled their past success. From 2000 to 2005, every time Blockbuster added a new store, their sales and profits increased. Their rapidly growing sales gave them progressively more power in negotiating favourable usage deals with movie producers and game developers. This success made them complacent, leading them to fix their mindset on what made them successful.

One of the best explanations of this I have come across is from the course, **Leading in the Digital Age by Boston University**. It summarises the change of mindset from industrial age mindset to the digital age mindset.

Shift of Mindset from Industrial Age Mindset to Digital Age Mindset

Mindset Factors	Industrial Age Mindset	Digital Age Mindset
Strategic Focus	Focus on producing standardised, high volume products to create economise of scale	Anticipating customers' changing preferences, problems and needs to be the first toprovide solutions that improve their customer experience
Basis for Managing / Leading	Formal authority granted by the organisation to managers to direct and conotrl their workers	Trust earned by demonstrating trustworthiness while leading teams to achieve a common goal and produce mutual value
Structure	A rigid functional hierarchy in which managers implemented top-down plans thorugh tightly defined tasks, using assets owned and controlled by the organsation	A value network of competent, creative, professionals, empowered to make decisions and inovate within their organisation's strategic intent, cultural values and operating principles, integrating their partners' capabiltiies and resoruces with their own.
Collaboration	No collaboration - each worker is responsible for completing their defines tasks as specified with minimal or no discussion.	High collaboration occurs through a network across units, functionsa and organisations to apply yhe best capabilities to co-create value.
Role of Information	Information is captured and pushed through the hierarchy top the top managers for decision making; the information is then protected as a corporate asset for internal and external reporting	Information is captured in the cloud and used wherever it is needed to enable dynamic learning and gain insights which are shard across the organisation to adjust, improve and continously innovate.

Apart from the shift in mindset, where leaders need to be able to think and act differently, leaders also need to be agile and comfortable with uncertainty as discussed in Chapter 3. Being digitally savvy is important as leaders need to leverage technology and data to drive decision making.

Leading a team in the digital era will also require a new skillset which requires leaders to collaborate and build relationships across different departments and functions. They also need to be able to lead cross-functional teams, manage virtual teams as well as manage teams from external organisations as part of collaborating in an ecosystem. Co-creation and ecosystem in Chapter 7.

Additionally, leaders must build and manage a digitally led culture to be successful in this digital era. They should be able to create an environment where employees feel empowered to make decisions and solve problems using technology and data. Leaders also need to foster an innovative culture, where employees are encouraged to try new things.

Next, let us look at an important culture for organisations to compete in the current digital era.

'In-Out' versus 'Out-In'

"In-Out" and "Out-In" organisations are two different approaches to how organisations are set up to operate and with different leadership styles.

With an In-Out organisation, the focus is to identify and leverage the company's strengths and capabilities, such as efficient processes, effective protocols, talented employees, and supply side economies of scale to create a product based not on a market need but on a belief in the product's potential as a desirable good. With an In-out strategy, you look at how to maximise these resources so you can create a valuable product or service that you can then market to potential customers.

The Out-In strategy does not start with an organisation's strengths, but with asking what consumers want. An Out-In organisation fills in the market gaps when consumers want something that existing products and services do not offer. Research is the first step an Out-In strategy to understand the market an organisation wants to reach. This forces a business to view the market from a consumer's perspective and create a product or service where its value is evident. It is driven by insights and feedback from front-line employees and customers. This approach is often associated with a more decentralised and agile structure.

As organisations fight to stay relevant and react quickly to rapidly changing market conditions, adopting an Out-In culture and leadership style becomes increasingly important. With such a culture, collaboration, teamwork, and tapping into collective intelligence are emphasised. In order achieve this, the organisation will have to empower its employees, leverage technology and data, and create a culture of innovation and continuous improvement.

Whether an organisation chooses to implement the In-Out or Out-In strategy depends greatly on the organisation's specific needs and goals, but the latter seems to be becoming more popular in the digital age as organisations strive to become more agile, responsive, and customer-focused. Most organisations will fall somewhere between the In-Out and Out-In approach. While outward-facing functions like marketing, sales, business development, and customer experience management need to adopt Out-In thinking, management roles like HR, finance, planning, and operations need to consider both In-Out and Out-In strategies. The best organisations skilfully employ both approaches.

Value Network Organisations (VNOs)

In the digital era, the concept of Value Network Organisations (VNOs) is becoming important. Let us dive into what a VNO is, and why it is considered a more beneficial organisational structure than a functional organisation.

VNO is an organisation that prioritises value creation and delivery over traditional hierarchical and functional structures. A VNO works as a network and has teams focused on customers or markets, instead of being organised into departments and functions. It is the goal of a VNO to bring together the resources and expertise that will deliver value to customers as efficiently and effectively as possible.

VNOs allow a company to be more responsive to the ever-evolving market conditions and customer's needs. VNOs can quickly pivot and adapt to changing customer needs by breaking down silos and encouraging cross-functional teamwork. In the fast-paced, highly competitive business environment of today, organisations need to be able to respond quickly and effectively to new opportunities and challenges.

To illustrate the benefit of adapting to changes in market conditions quickly, let us look at a real-life example of Nvidia's brilliant strategy to establish three separate development teams to each work on an eighteen-month start-to-market cycle which was the industry norm. This meant that with overlapping schedules, the three teams would deliver a new product every six-months. The benefit of a faster cycle is that the product will be best in class more often. Compared to a competitor working on an eighteen-month cycle, Nvidia's six-month cycle would mean that its chip would be the better product about 83% of the time. In addition, there would be constant buzz surrounding new product introductions.

Innovation and continuing improvement are also advantages of a VNO. VNOs encourage a culture of innovation that fosters creativity that helps organisations stay ahead of the curve by removing traditional hierarchies and empowering employees to collaborate and make decisions. VNOs also promote a customer-centric approach because they put the customer at the centre of everything the company does.

To be able to lead in a VNO, there is a need for leadership to develop a new skill set. The ability to not only lead teams in a specific function but also teams from different functions, external organisations and potentially from different geographical locations are vital.

Functional organisations, on the other hand, are often separated by different departments or functions, and each department has a specific set of goals and responsibilities. The functional organisation structure can be effective in some situations, but it can also lead to silos and lack of cross-functional collaboration. Employees, therefore, are more focused on their own departmental goals than on the organisation's overall success, which means they are not responsive to customer needs.

Another downside of a functional organisation is that they can lead to slow decision-making and implementation. Because decisions often need to be made and approved by multiple departments, it can take a long time for initiatives to be implemented, which can result in missed opportunities and increased costs. In contrast, VNOs encourage a more decentralised and agile approach allowing decisions to be made quickly and efficiently at the point of value creation. We will discuss the Lean & Agile approach in more detail in the next chapter.

Overall, VNOs offer several benefits over traditional functional organisations. By breaking down silos and encouraging collaboration, VNOs can be more responsive to customer needs and the rapidly changing market conditions, while also fostering innovation and continuous improvement. Additionally, VNOs encourage a customer-centric approach that puts the customer at the centre of everything the organisation does, which is essential for a business to succeed.

A VNO structure may be the right choice for your organisation if you want to improve your organisation's competitiveness, innovation, or customer focus. There is no one-size-fits-all approach to organisational design, but if you want to stay competitive in today's fast-paced business environment, a VNO might be the way to go. Consideration must be given to leadership skills and ensuring that the organisation has the right skill set to transform into this new culture.

Ford

Ford Motor Company has a long history of excellence in HR and leadership practices. The company was founded in 1903 and has since become one of the largest automakers in the world. Over the years, Ford has consistently demonstrated its commitment to its employees through a variety of HR policies and practices, as well as its focus on fostering a culture of leadership. Before we dive into its people strategy, let us look back at a little of Ford's history.

Founded in 1903, Henry Ford quickly became a leader in innovation, leading his company to become one of the world's largest automakers. The company made big profits for decades, but as we know, success is not always permanent or guaranteed. In 2006, it was clear that things were starting to change. Ford was struggling, because of rising labour costs, declining market share, and a bunch of other problems. The company made the biggest loss ever in that year – $12.7 billion. When Alan Mulally became CEO in September of that year, he said immediately that turnaround plans were already in the works.

Mullaly had a business strategy called the 'One Ford' strategy. This business strategy focuses on the company's growth and innovation by producing quality, safe, and diversified products that will be able it to penetrate the global market (Ford Motor Company, 2017). Mulally's One Ford innovation platform consisted of four main areas:

1. Bring all Ford employees together as a global team;
2. Leverage Ford's unique automotive knowledge and assets;
3. Build cars and trucks that people wanted and valued;
4. Arrange the significant financing necessary to pay for it all.

Increased sales combined with fewer disparate platforms meant greater efficiency and greater margins. But the turnaround wasn't just financial, and wasn't just about efficiency. 'One Ford' also meant creating a culture of innovation,' - Allan Mullaly, Ford CEO

He started cross-functional teams and an open-minded culture. In a town hall meeting, he famously claimed, ***'We've been going out of business for 40 years.'*** Employees rallied around the turnaround effort as a result of bold decisions and an open culture. More than 45,000 workers are still employed because the union negotiated lower pay. The culture of collaboration and innovation led to important product changes that led the industry.

Ford recognised the importance of diversity and inclusion as an integral part of its people strategy. They understood that it was crucial to the company's success. This led to the company setting up programmes and initiatives to ensure that it is promoted at every level in the organisation. Hiring, training and developing a diverse pool of talented workforce received a lot of attention together with promoting diversity and inclusion. The company's retention and hiring plan was to employ innovative and customer centric minds while retaining and promoting those who were skilled.

Employee engagement and development was another focus of Ford's people strategy. The company recognised the importance of keeping its employees motivated and engaged in order to maintain a high level of productivity and satisfaction. In order to achieve this, Ford provides its employees with a range of opportunities which includes professional growth, training and development programmes, mentoring and coaching sessions, and recognition for performance-based achievements.

Ford has always prioritised developing and promoting strong leaders within the organisation. Company leadership programmes are designed to develop talented individuals in making them effective leaders within the organisation. These programs provide individuals with the skills and knowledge they need to succeed. One example is the Marketing Leadership Programme which redefined the way marketing is strategically implemented within its core automotive business and emerging mobility units. The Marketing Leadership Programme (MLP) is designed to launch the careers of Ford's future marketing leaders with riveting assignments, a diverse network, and accelerated advancement opportunities. Since its inception in 1989, this MBA-focused rotational programme has produced dozens of dedicated senior executives and continues to develop the marketing leaders of tomorrow.

Most MLP participants begin their journey at Ford as a summer intern, with a project based in one of their key marketing disciplines across a variety of exciting business units. After graduating from business school, full-time positions consist of three impactful rotations tailored to the employee's career goals.

Another example is the Ford Business Leader Programme (FBLP). The Ford Business Leader programme develops the general management capabilities necessary to manage the profit and loss of a business, market or product line within the company. Created in 2016, the FBLP is a cross-functional general management programme that provides participants with a unique opportunity to accelerate professional development and to position themselves as Ford Motor Company's future executive leaders. These future leaders create a platform for change; inspire, educate, and guide others. This competitive programme is open to candidates from top MBA programs who demonstrate an ability to excel at a global business level.

Apart from leadership programmes, Ford also places emphasis on employees' health and safety. Ford is committed to providing its employees with a safe and healthy work environment. There are a few programmes and initiatives which are designed to promote occupational health and safety, well-being of employees including physical health, mental health and work -life balance. In 1941, Ford started a collaboration with United Auto Workers (UAW) to enhance the health and safety of its workforce, both on and off the job. Ford and the UAW are leaders in developing a broad range of approaches to worker involvement and labour-management cooperation. These efforts, which have expanded and deepened over the years, have helped transform the company in many ways. They have helped Ford plants gain recognition for being among the most productive in the world, and they have contributed to increased market share, improved economic performance, and enhanced employee development and work satisfaction.

Ford is an organisation who values its people. It is a leader in HR and leadership practices and has shown commitment to its employees. It has focused on ensuring that its policies and initiatives encourage diversity and inclusion, employee engagement and development, leadership development, sustainability, and health and safety.

If you would like to delve deeper into understanding what is needed to lead in the digital era and the topic of Mindset, I recommend the following:

Recommended reading: Mindset: The New Psychology of Success, by Carol S. Dweck.

Recommended course: Leading in the Digital Age, edX by Boston University.

> **'Surround yourself with people that are smarter than you. Managers may view themselves differently than their employees view them, so it's important to constantly seek feedback and self-reflect. Leaders who seek feedback will not only grow; they will also end up with more satisfied teams'.**
>
> - Mark Fields, CEO, Ford, who oversees a company with more than 200,000 workers and 67 plants worldwide

Contribution by Nur Hamurcu, Managing Director at &samhoud Asia

'Digital is the main reason why over half of the Fortune 5 companies have disappeared since the year 2000.'

— Pierre Nanterme, CEO of Accenture

'The big moment for an organisation is when they have embraced the fact that digital transformation is not a technical issue but a cultural change. And, culture change is a pre-requisite for digital transformation.'

— Ian Rogers, Chief Digital Officer of LVMH

Everyone wants to go digital! Digital is not just a thing that you can buy and plug into the organisation. It is multi-faceted, diffused, and does not just involve technology. In fact, digital transformation is more than just about being digital; it is about remodelling businesses to be more agile, innovative and customer centric at its core. Digital transformation is an ongoing process of changing the way we do business.

It requires foundational investments in skills, projects, infrastructure, and often, in cleaning up IT systems. It requires mixing people, machines and business processes, with all of the messiness that it entails.

Hurdles to Digital Transformation

Digital transformation is the integration of technology into every aspect of a business or organisation. It has become an essential strategy for companies looking to stay competitive and innovative. However, despite the vast benefits, digital transformation can bring, many organisations fail to execute it successfully. One of the primary reasons for this failure is people and culture issues.

People and culture are at the heart of any organisation, and they play a crucial role in the success or failure of digital transformation initiatives. It is essential to understand that digital transformation is not just about technology. It involves a fundamental shift in the way an organisation operates, interacts with its customers, and approaches its work. Therefore, to achieve successful digital transformation, organisations must focus on their people and culture.

As Deborah Ancona, MIT Sloan School Professor noted, **'Leadership often underestimates the importance of culture.' Yet, an organisation's culture is one of the most prominent sources of its competitiveness.**

Without laying a strong foundation for culture and without the alignment of employees towards a digital vision, it will be extremely difficult to make anything meaningful; nor will there be any progress made on digital transformation.

Here are some other reasons why digital transformation fails due to people and culture issues:

Resistance to change

The lack of clarity and uncertainty are the biggest barriers to the success of digital transformation. People are naturally resistant to change, and when it comes to digital transformation, they may fear the unknown or feel uncomfortable with the new technology. In addition, people may feel that their jobs are at risk due to the implementation of new technologies.

Therefore, it is essential to involve employees in the process of digital transformation, provide them with the necessary training, and communicate with them effectively about the changes.

Lack of a clear vision and strategy

Digital transformation is a complex and multi-dimensional process that requires a clear vision and strategy. However, many organizations may not have a well-defined vision or strategy for digital transformation. Without a clear vision and strategy, it can be challenging to align people, processes, and technology towards a common goal, which can result in failure.

Lack of leadership commitment and support

Digital transformation is a significant change that requires strong leadership support. However, many leaders may not understand the importance of digital transformation or may not be willing to invest the necessary time and resources. Leaders must be committed to the digital transformation process and communicate the benefits and objectives of the initiative to the entire organisation. They must also provide the necessary resources, such as funding and technology, to support the process.

Lack of skills and training

Digital transformation requires employees to acquire new skills and knowledge to use new technologies effectively. However, many organisations fail to provide adequate training and support to their employees. This can lead to employees feeling overwhelmed, frustrated, and resistant to change. Organisations must invest in training and development programmes to ensure their employees are equipped with the necessary skills to succeed in the digital age.

Silos and lack of collaboration

Digital transformation requires a collaborative approach that involves breaking down silos and working across teams and departments. However, many organisations are structured in a way that promotes silos, which can hinder collaboration and innovation. To achieve a successful digital transformation, organisations must create a culture of collaboration and encourage cross-functional teams to work together towards a common goal.

In conclusion, digital transformation can bring tremendous benefits to organisations, but it is not without its challenges. People and culture issues are one of the primary reasons why digital transformations fail. Successful digital transformation, can be achieved if organisations focus on their people and culture, involve employees in the process, provide adequate training and support, ensure strong leadership support, break down silos, and have a clear True North. By doing so, organisations can transform themselves and stay competitive in the digital age.

07

Lean & Agile Approach

The Lean and Agile concepts are not new concepts in the business world. These two approaches to how a business is managed, emphasises speed, flexibility and a focus on customer. In this chapter, we will look into the importance of these two concepts and how they can help companies achieve their goals.

Let us begin with the Lean concept. Although there are instances of rigorous process thinking in manufacturing all the way back to the Arsenal in Venice in the 1450s, the first person to truly integrate an entire production process was Henry Ford. At Highland Park, MI, in 1913 he married consistently interchangeable parts with standard work and moving conveyance to create what he called flow production. The public grasped this in the dramatic form of the moving assembly line, but from the standpoint of the manufacturing engineer the breakthroughs went much further.

The term 'Lean manufacturing' was coined in 1991 and many of its principles were formalised in The Machine That Changed the World by James P. Womack, Daniel T. Jones, and Daniel Roos of MIT and in Lean Thinking (1996) by the same authors based on their observations at Toyota.

It was created to help the company increase efficiency and eliminate waste in its production process. Today, Lean is used by organisations of all sizes, from small start-ups to large corporations, to streamline their operations and create a more agile, customer-focused business.

Lean thinking is a system used in management that includes ideas, actions and principles which help to enhance effectiveness and the standard of work. It promotes collaboration throughout the whole organisation with an aim to arrange human activities for greater societal benefit and value while getting rid of excess. The five fundamentals of the lean methodology are Value, Value Stream, Flow, Pull and Perfection.

Value – Understand what customers value in a product or service.

Value Stream – What goes into maximising value and eliminating waste throughout the entire process from design to production.

Flow – All product processes flow and synchronises seamlessly with one another.

Pull – Flow is made possible by 'pull', or the idea that nothing is made before it is needed, thereby creating shorter delivery cycles.

Perfection – Relentlessly pursue perfection by constantly engaging the problem-solving process.

Basically, the goal is to make things run smoother on the inside so that customers get highest value possible in a product or service. Anything that does not add value for them is seen as a waste of time and resources.

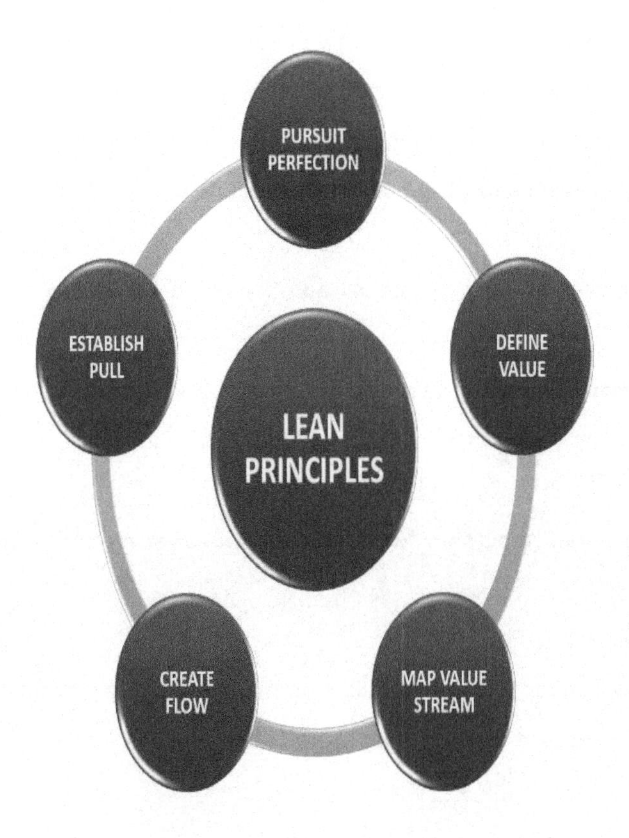

Let us now understand the Agile concept. It was first developed in the software industry in the spring of 2000, when a group of 17 software developers, including Martin Fowler, Jim Highsmith, Jon Kern, Jeff Sutherland, Ken Schwaber, and Bob Martin met in Oregon to discuss how they could speed up development times in order bring new software to market faster. Today, Agile is used by organisations across a wide range of industries, from tech to finance to retail.

The Agile methodology is mainly about how flexible an organisation is and how they can quickly adapt to change. It is a way to manage projects that makes it easier for teams to give customers what they want quicker. Instead of going all-in on one big launch, an agile team releases work in smaller pieces that are still useful. This allows them to respond quickly to changes in the market and customer needs, and to make course corrections along the way.

The Agile approach gets the team focused on what is important to the project. It helps eliminate long, bureaucratic processes. When the Agile method is adopted, teams usually work together quickly and creatively and focus on delivering value to the customers. This approach has four overarching values – Unity, Simplicity, Transparency and Adaptability.

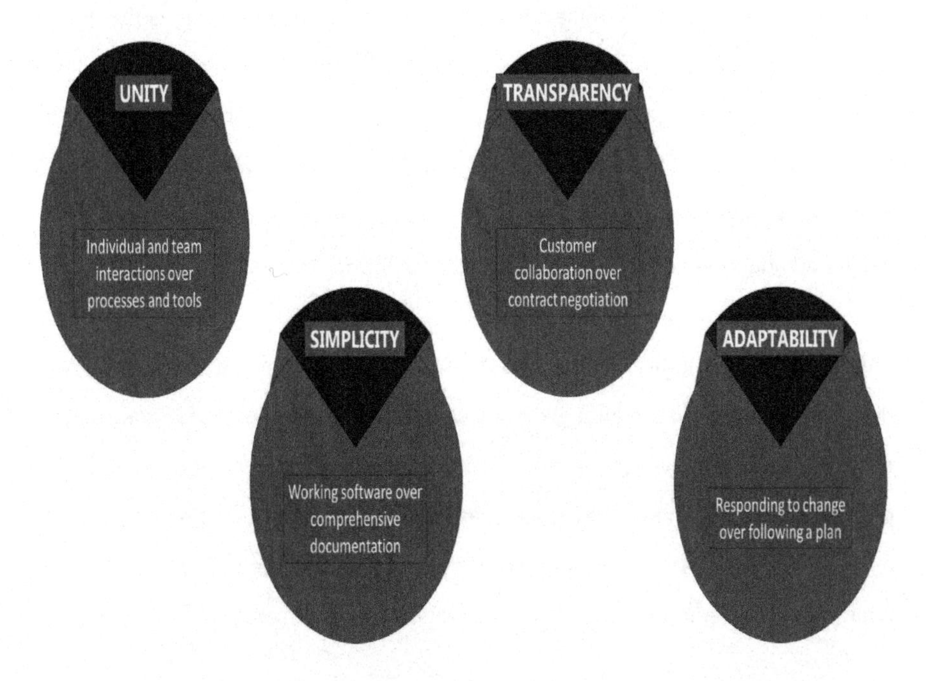

With a basic understanding of the Lean and Agile principles, let's understand why they are important in today's increasingly complex and fast paced business world we operate in. It has become vital that organisations are able to adapt quickly to changing customer demands, technology and business environments. By embracing the Lean and Agile principles, it allows businesses to become more responsive, more focused on the customer and remain competitive.

Some of the benefits of applying the Lean methodology are:

Reduced bottlenecks – With the Lean approach, the team keeps track of how much they can handle and what tasks are in progress. This way, the team will know when there might be problems ahead of time and everyone works together to avoid wasting anyone's time.

Improving productivity and efficiency – By applying Lean concepts in your business, processes that don't provide customer value are eliminated, therefore, the team can dedicate its energy exclusively to the processes that do, which leads to increasing the team's value flow, efficiency and productivity.

Cost reduction – Adopting the Lean methodology means increasing efficiency, which benefits any company's bottom line. The selling price is impacted by various factors that could determine or be determined by product quality, attributes, and markets. Lean methodology helps in controlling or eliminating costs that don't add value.

Increased adaptability – Using Lean concepts, teams can better adapt quickly. Lean systems aren't as rigid and allows adjustments along the way, meaning teams will better adjust for unexpected circumstances.

Stakeholder visibility and strong customer relationships – With Lean, customer value is key, and every project and task begins with considering the customer's point of view of. Feedback is gathered alongside product development instead of at the end to ensure new information is considered and regularly incorporated. This results in quick course correction and a final product will be exactly what the customer needs or wants.

Continuous improvement mindset – Being Lean means you're always looking for ways to make things better and not settling for the way things are. It's all about continuously improving processes and having a mindset that embraces change.

Increased team engagement – Lean organisations, puts teams on the frontline of product development. Under Lean management, employees have direct and regular contact with managers about how their work is going and how the process could be improved. Teams are more open to improvement and are looking for ways to consistently make the work they do even more impactful.

Promote innovation – It can also help free up resources that can be invested in growth and innovation.

The Agile methodology when implemented, can make teams collaborate better, leading to quicker project completion and improved results. Some of the benefits of the Agile concept are:

More flexibility – Agile is all about being flexible. Agile teams are quick to adapt and can handle changes without causing too much chaos. They don't stick rigidly to their plans, so they can easily adjust their goals as needed. This flexibility helps them deliver what clients want and manage changing requirements with ease.

More control – Making small improvements along the way is super important for both the team and customer. You can divide tasks into chunks and tackle them quickly in regular standups. Meetings happen often with agile, so everyone knows how things are going, talks about issues and comes up with fixes together. Plus, it makes everything clearer as you go through it all step by step.

Increased predictability – Agile teams work in short time periods, sometimes referred to as sprints. These fixed durations (e.g. two weeks) make it easier for project managers to measure team performance and assign resources accordingly. It is also easier to predict costs for shorter time periods than for a long-term project, simplifying the estimation process.

Products of superior quality – The incremental nature of the agile method (iterative approach) means that projects are completed in shorter sprints, making them more manageable. It also allows products to be rolled out quickly and changes to be easily made at any point during the process.

Decreased risk – Developers regularly assess progress during sprints, meaning they have better visibility into the project and can spot potential obstacles quickly. These minor issues can be tackled before they escalate, creating an effective risk mitigation process and giving the project a greater chance of success.

Satisfied customer – Close collaboration between the project team and the customer provides immediate feedback. The customer can make tweaks to their expectations and desires throughout the process. These tailor-made deliverables will likely improve the overall user experience and boost customer retention.

Lean and Agile are not just about getting stuff done faster. They are also about building a culture where the team is always looking to make things better, and where everyone has the power to be part of that process. When businesses embrace these approaches, it creates a great work atmosphere – one where people feel respected and excited to help the company succeed.

How do you start implementing the Lean and Agile concepts in your organisation? The first step is to fully understand the principles. At the end of this chapter, I have recommended a book to further understand the Lean methodology. Once you have a good understanding of the concepts, you can start small, perhaps by implementing Lean or Agile in one small part of the organisation.

This will give you a chance to see how the principles work in practice and make any necessary adjustments before rolling it out more broadly. Leadership also plays a crucial role. For Lean and Agile to work, leaders must fully believe in the principles and be open to tweaking their leadership styles when needed.

Toyota

Toyota is an exemplary organisation that has been at the forefront of business transformation for several decades. They were pioneers in embracing and implementing Lean principles, which paved the way for their continued success as leaders in Agile methodology adoption. We will explore Toyota's successful transformation strategy by examining how they incorporated both Lean and Agile principles to achieve remarkable results.

Let us start with Lean. Toyota developed a new concept of 'lean manufacturing' in the early 20th century. The company recognised that holding inventory incurred significant production costs and addressed this problem by minimising waste, particularly excessive materials. This led to the creation of an efficient business model that prioritised customer satisfaction – known today as lean production. The development of the Toyota Production System was influenced by various factors including Japan's strong work ethic which emphasises perfectionism across all domains. Moreover, Ford had a noteworthy impact on Toyota's adoption of lean concepts owing to valuable lessons learned from studying their practices. Ultimately, implementing Lean principles became intrinsic to Toyota's culture and operations contributing significantly towards its longstanding success.

Continuous improvement is a fundamental principle of Lean methodology, which Toyota adopts. This implies that the organisation consistently seeks to enhance its operations and minimise waste production. As a result, it has managed to outperform rivals and sustain its dominance in the automotive industry.

An illustration of Lean's effectiveness can be seen through Toyota's implementation, which resulted in a streamlined supply chain that has reduced costs and enhanced efficiency. The company was also able to lower inventory levels and swiftly adapt to shifts in customer demands with the help of Lean principles. By incorporating these principles into their business model, Toyota established an agile and customer-oriented approach that kept them competitive amidst constant market changes.

Though maintaining low inventory levels is an essential aspect of Lean Manufacturing, it is not the only one. Equally significant are the fundamental pillars of this system that do not require advanced technology but rely on strict compliance with procedures, continuous improvement through the Kaizen approach, root cause analysis and recognition for line workers' contributions.

Toyota executives emphasise that their system's success lies in utilising team members' knowledge and perspectives while providing them comprehensive training opportunities and responsibilities. By harnessing employees' creativity, Toyota can consistently enhance its operations.

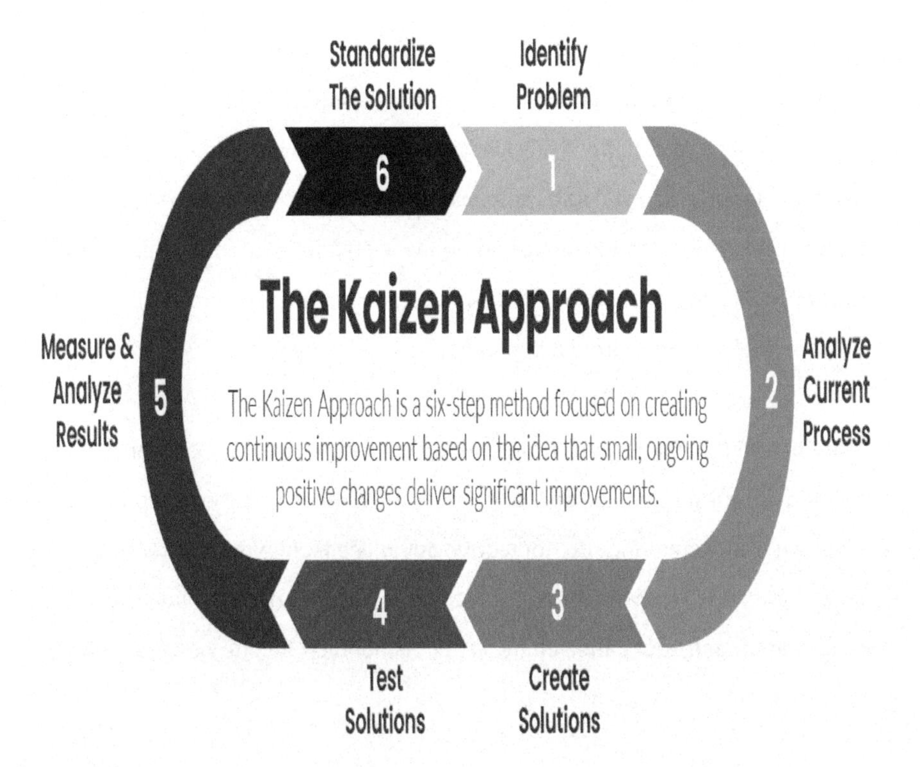

Let's talk about Agile. It is a way of managing projects that started in the software world. Toyota embraced it because they can use it to be more productive and react faster when customers want something different. For instance, if someone wants changes made to a project, Toyota make them quickly thanks to Agile. This keeps them ahead of everyone else and lets them stay on top as the standard bearer in the automotive world.

One of the key benefits of Agile at Toyota is that it has helped the company to develop products more quickly and with higher quality. By working in short sprints, Toyota can deliver small pieces of a project incrementally which allows them to make course corrections along the way and respond quickly to changes in customer demand. Toyota has found that Agile helps create an environment of constant betterment. With quick work cycles, teams stay on track and cooperate as teammates. It has made working there feel more inclusive, with everyone having a part in achieving success.

A fundamental principle at Toyota is 'stop and fix' which literally meant for Toyota to stop the production line as soon as a quality problem was detected, apply the *'five whys' technique to find the root cause of the problem, mitigate (not find the perfect solution) and then resume the production line.

The 'stop and fix' principle also had a second purpose: to force continuous learning. In general, adults, or at least a great number of us, do not want to continue learning and therefore a practice like this forced Toyota developers to stop working, reflect on what was not working well, propose possible mitigations and experiment with them.

There are a few reasons why the transformation at Toyota was successful. For a start, they got on board with the Lean and Agile ways early on which kept them ahead of their competition and in front as leaders of the automotive industry. Secondly, they embraced the concepts as part of their culture (to be Lean and Agile) – this helped make them more customer-focused and adaptable as a business. Finally, by always trying to improve themselves over time has allowed them to stay ahead in a disruptive, ever-evolving market.

Toyota has done a great job of using the Lean and Agile methodology as part of their transformation strategy and this is one of the reasons of why they have been able to stay ahead in the automotive industry. Additionally, it has helped them to become more focused on customers and to adapt quickly to changes in the industry and technology. It is a great learning experience from Toyota, and applying these principles to your strategy, could make a big difference to your business!

PayPal

The PayPal team made a big move by transforming their whole system through a strategy called the Big Bang Agile. It was during the early 2010s when they were dealing with several problems like sluggish decision-making and overlooking customers' needs. In order to deal with these issues, they implemented an Agile transformation process in their company.

PayPal's 'Big Bang' Agile transformation was a significant effort to shift the company's culture and processes toward an Agile methodology. The four pillars of this transformation are as follows:

Customer-centricity – This pillar emphasised the importance of putting the customer at the centre of all decision-making processes. The Agile approach emphasises customer feedback, continuous delivery, and constant improvement based on customer input.

According to Kirsten Wolberg, Vice President of Technology Business Operations at PayPal, who stated in an article (Techtarget), 'The first pillar, was around customer-driven innovation or CDI. This brings into the development process that key connection with the customer: So, asking the customer what is the problem that we are trying to solve and injecting continuous customer input and customer feedback into the development process.'

Product model and Accountability – The second pillar emphasised individual and team accountability. Teams were given autonomy and empowered to make decisions, but they were also held responsible for the outcomes of their decisions.

Wolberg: So, the second pillar is developing a product model. Historically, PayPal has been sort of project-driven, meaning they put projects together and that project launched a product and then they moved on to the next project. We broke that paradigm and introduced a product-line discipline. We identified 17 independent product lines and then 35 sub-x` are an engineer, you will persist as a member of a team that is working on a given product line. That way we make sure to really develop the accountability, the ownership and the pride of craftsmanship around building a product and building exceptional customer experiences.

Agile Delivery Methodology – The third pillar was to transition from waterfall methodology to Agile.

*Wolberg: Within PayPal when I got here we had probably 20% to 25% of teams working in some form of Agile. But the rest of the organization was a Waterfall delivery methodology. Given how quickly we wanted to move and given how responsive we needed to be as we were now getting customer input and feedback, the Waterfall methodology was breaking down. It was also breaking down because those teams that were working in Agile were relying on other teams that were working in *Waterfall and the handoffs and handshakes just weren't happening in a way that was giving us the ability to have high levels of productivity. It was really frustrating for the engineers. So, we brought in the Agile delivery model and we are now using Agile across 510 teams and in all of our locations. We had essentially a big bang, where we went from about 20% Agile to 100% of our teams being able to work within Agile.*

** Waterfall methodology is a widely used project management method with a linear approach. In Waterfall, each stage of the workflow needs to be completed before moving on to the next step. While there are various types of project management methodologies, Waterfall is well suited for projects where the objectives are clearly outlined from the beginning.*

Employee engagement – The fourth pillar focused on creating a positive and engaging work environment that fostered innovation and creativity. This involved providing opportunities for skill development, encouraging collaboration, and recognising and rewarding achievement.

Wolberg: We had a transformation team of over 110 people across the organization. Each of those individuals was doing this not as their full-time job, but in addition to what their day job was. So, we didn't hire up an additional 110 people; we got passionate volunteers to work with us going above and beyond in order to help drive this transformation. I had a small group of individuals on my team of about 10 people who worked full time and were dedicated to this. But essentially, they are the enterprise resources that we put against any enterprise transformation, and this is where we focused those resources and will focus those resources for the duration.

Together, these four pillars formed the foundation of PayPal's Big Bang Agile transformation, enabling the company to become more agile, customer-focused, and innovative.

Overall, the Big Bang Agile transformation at PayPal was a major success. The company was able to address many of the challenges it was facing, and it was able to become a much more customer-focused organisation. The Agile approach helped PayPal to be more responsive to customer needs, and it allowed the company to make decisions more quickly and effectively.

Big Bang Agile transformation at PayPal serves as a great illustration of the benefits that can be achieved through a large-scale Agile transformation. The key to the success of the transformation was the level of buy-in from employees, as well as the training and support that were provided. If you are considering an Agile transformation, it is important to keep these factors in mind to ensure that your transformation is a success.

The book by Eric Ries, The Lean Startup is a great read to get a better understanding of the Lean concept.

08

Co-creation & Ecosystem

Digital transformation has become an essential part of every industry as it has enabled businesses to gain a competitive edge. However, digital transformation is not just about adopting new technologies, but it also requires a shift in organisational culture, processes, and partnerships. Culture is shaped by the changing mindsets of business leaders in embracing and investing in newer technologies to boost growth and resilience. Leaders must take the first steps towards innovation by resourcing teams to experiment, test and validate new digital technologies towards the goal of adopting them. Processes have enabled the leaders to manifest and embed this change in culture into business operations to realise the intended results.

While culture and processes are internal to a business, it cannot remain isolated from the external environment within which it operates. Therefore, partnerships and ecosystems play an equally vital role in facilitating digital transformation. We will discuss the role of partnerships and ecosystems in the digital transformation in greater detail.

Partnerships

Collaboration with technology providers, vendors, startups and industry players is crucial for organisations to achieve mutual goals in the digital transformation process. Partnerships can take different forms like co-development agreements, strategic alliances or joint ventures enabling a business to innovate further. For instance, an enterprise focused on manufacturing could team up with IoT service providers toward developing smart factories optimised through sensor technologies. Alternatively, partnering with AI startups towards creating inspection stations that capitalise on artificial intelligence systems which cater both as production lines site-based control, guarantees quality measures and by combining efforts for go-to-market commercialisation, initiatives would emerge drastically wider than going solo.

Incorporating partnerships into an organisation's operations facilitates access to fresh expertise skills and promising new ways of operation, which otherwise may not be available with in-house resources during said firm's journey into digitisation -therefore fastening innovational breakthroughs.

Undertaking digital transformation can also pose as a financial challenge for organisations, with many lacking the necessary resources to fund it independently. Thus, partnering up assists in cost-sharing and risk distribution, providing more feasibility in validating the required investment.

Ecosystem

Ecosystems are interconnected networks of organisations, startups, investors, regulators and other stakeholders that work together to co-create value. They enable organisations to create new business models and revenue streams. For example, a manufacturing company may partner with a fintech startup to develop a cloud manufacturing platform with secure payment gateways based on smart contracts that allows customers to make payments for their parts once they are produced as per the validated and audited quality requirements.

This new platform creates a new revenue stream for the manufacturing company and enables it to gain a competitive edge vis-à-vis other players in the market. Furthermore, ecosystems also enable organisations to access new markets and customers. By partnering with startups and other players in the ecosystem, organisations can tap into new customer segments and markets that they may not have been able to reach on their own.

Open Innovation

Open innovation is the practice of businesses and organisations sourcing ideas from external sources as well as internal ones. This means sharing knowledge and information about problems and looking to people outside the business for solutions and suggestions. In practice, open innovation can take the form of established partnerships like Delphi and Mobileye working on autonomous driving systems, through to co-creation competitions and hackathons like the BMW startup challenge, and crowdsourcing portals like the Unilever's and 'My Starbucks Idea' platform.

Instead of the secrecy and silo mentality of traditional business R&D, open innovation invites a wider group of people to participate in problem-solving and product development. Open innovation isn't just a one-way street, either. By inviting others to participate in generating ideas for products and services, companies can also share information and expertise with communities of fans and customers. This way, the pool of ideas is expanded, innovation costs are lowered and the lead time to market is shrunk.

In conclusion, partnerships, ecosystems and open innovation play a critical role in the digital transformation of the industry. Partnerships enable organisations to access new technologies and expertise, share the costs and risks of digital transformation, and create new business models and revenue streams. Ecosystems enable organisations to access new markets and customers, collaborate with other players in the ecosystem, and create value through innovation.

Open Innovation enables organisations to tap into the external networks for idea generation and solutioning thereby supplementing internal innovation capabilities and capacities with lower costs and faster time to market. As digital transformation continues to accelerate, partnerships, ecosystems and open innovation will become even more critical for organisations that want to stay ahead of the competition and drive growth.

Role of Higher Education Institutes

Collaboration with higher education institutions plays an enabling role in facilitating partnerships for digital transformation. With the industry's rapid digitisation, there arises an increasing need for competent professionals who are capable of spearheading and overseeing digital transformation endeavors. Working alongside industries, tertiary education providers can impart essential learning and skills necessary to cultivate expertise in this field.

Higher education institutions can collaborate with industry professionals to create courses and programs that highlight digital transformation skills. This partnership would identify the most desired abilities and knowledge in this field, allowing them to adapt their coursework accordingly. By participating in internships, work experiences, and collaborative projects within these industries, students will be exposed to current technologies as well as possible trends making them a valuable candidate for prospective employers through practical experience applying existing knowledge on real-world settings. Additionally, higher education institutions may establish innovation centers partnered with industry experts for research advancements and application enhancements leading towards excellence through technological contributions across varied sectors of society.

Through these centres, they can identify emerging trends and technologies in the industry and co-develop new solutions and digital enabled processes to address the challenges faced by industry players with active participation from students and faculty. While students are clear beneficiaries, the active involvement by faculty will ensure that the teaching staff remain relevant by maintaining their skills currency in tune with the industry which in turn will enable them to infuse the latest technological and process know-how into the course curricula.

An example of higher education institutes partnering with the industry to drive digital transformation is Nanyang Polytechnic (NYP) in Singapore. The polytechnic offers full time pre-employment training programmes and part time continuing education and training programmes in multiple disciplines to secondary school leavers and adult learners respectively. It collaborates with global technology companies such as HP, SAS and Nvidia in training courses and certifications to infuse the latest digital technologies and industry know-how into its curricula which is competency based. Students work on industry projects through their entire course, participate in technology competitions and industry hackathons, undertake dedicated full time internships and even take customised study pathways to accommodate short industry experience stints in Singapore and overseas. The polytechnic also establishes centres of innovation and excellence in partnership with global technology leaders an example of which is the NYP-Microsoft Centre for Applied AI (C4AI).

This centre in partnership with Microsoft promotes the use of AI technologies across different industry sectors by developing and demonstrating exemplar use cases, providing development platforms and test beds for companies to experiment with AI, working with companies on joint R&D projects to co-develop new AI technologies and solutions and organising short training programmes and workshops for industry participants to upskill themselves with the latest AI and allied technology skillsets. The centre also enables companies to de-risk and lower the cost of AI adoption by helping them validate their use cases and justify their intended investments by working on projects with the centre and investing in adoption only upon successful experimentation and demonstration.

More higher education institutes like NYP are plugging into the industry-academia nexus and driving the symbiotic collaborations forward within the digital transformation ecosystem. These collaborations not only help companies accelerate their transformation efforts but also provides them with a pool of highly trained and skilled workforce which they have participated in creating. Countries which promote and nurture the industry-academia collaborations will emerge stronger over the long term, boosting their growth potential and global competitiveness.

Co-Creation

The process of digital transformation encompasses the incorporation of technology across various business domains, ranging from operational functions to customer engagement. This assimilation has resulted in companies reconsidering their strategies pertaining to interactions with stakeholders such as customers, partners, and other stakeholders.

And this is where the concept of ecosystems and co-creation comes in. An ecosystem as we have seen, refers to a network comprising interconnected entities that collaborate towards accomplishing a shared objective. In the context of digital transformation, an ecosystem encompasses clients, associates, vendors, and even competitors. The fundamental principle underlying this concept is that by collaborating with each other harmoniously, all parties involved can generate more value collectively than they could independently.

Why do we need co-creation for digital transformation? Customers and stakeholders are getting more empowered these days. They are much better informed and have tons of options to choose from. They, therefore, want companies to be more aware of their needs and wishes. This is where co-creation becomes important; it helps bridge the gap between businesses and people's expectations.

Embracing the process of co-creation is vital for companies seeking success in today's digital world. This involves collaborating with customers and other stakeholders to cultivate innovative ideas that lead to valuable products, services, and experiences. By tapping into collective intelligence within a community, businesses can leverage customer insights for optimal outcomes. Ultimately, adopting a co-creation approach will enhance brand loyalty and strengthen relationships with stakeholders.

Co-creation offers a valuable advantage to organisations as it facilitates the creation of products and services that are more relevant. Through close collaboration with customers, businesses can gain a deeper understanding of their demands and preferences. Consequently, they can develop personalised offerings that meet precise requirements leading to increased satisfaction levels among customers resulting in higher retention rates over time.

Engaging in co-creation not only benefits customers and stakeholders, but also helps companies maintain a competitive edge. With technology evolving at an unprecedented rate, it is virtually impossible for any one organisation to stay up to date alone. However, by collaborating with external parties through co-creation initiatives, businesses can take advantage of fresh insights and novel concepts that they may have overlooked otherwise. This fosters growth and development while positioning the company ahead of rivals within the industry.

How do companies go about co-creating with their customers and other stakeholders? There are a few key steps that companies can take to get started.

Listen to customers – To start the co-creation process, companies have to listen to their customers and get a feel for what they are into. They could do this by sending out surveys, having chat sessions with focus groups or just keeping an ear out for any feedback that comes in. Do not underestimate the importance of customer facing staff members as their daily interactions with customers can bring vital information on customer preferences. Establishing a good feedback loop from customer facing staff members can be very valuable.

Engage with customers – Companies must not only understand their customers' desires but also take proactive actions to actualise those ideas. The best way of achieving this goal is through inclusive customer engagement at every stage of the ideation process, such as co-creation workshops or hackathons. These collaborative efforts aim for one objective: surpassing customer expectations and providing unparalleled value. It is high time that businesses adopt these innovative approaches to transform how they interact with their clients.

Leverage the ecosystem partners – In addition to customers, working with partners in the ecosystem to help refine ideas and contribute to the product or service creation stage can help bring new insights and expertise that are not available in the organisation.

Prototype and test – To ensure that their ideas are feasible, companies should start by making prototypes and testing them. Co-creation is an iterative process, and it is important to continually refine the product based on feedback from the stakeholders. By doing small-scale trials or pilots, businesses can learn what works and does not work when introducing a new product or service. This is an efficient way to collect feedback from customers that could be used to improve the offering before releasing it on a larger scale. Consequently, prototyping and testing continue to be crucial elements of any business plan designed for long term success in today's competitive market.

Leverage technology – Embrace technology as your ally in fostering co-creation within an ecosystem. With a plethora of collaborative tools at our disposal, including project management software, online collaboration platforms and video conferencing facilities – we can seamlessly unite stakeholders and streamline the process of co-creation. Let us harness the power of these technological advancements to unlock limitless possibilities for innovation.

The illustration on the next page is an example of an ecosystem that was built for a large format retail organisation. It is not by means a complete ecosystem but shows how different stakeholders were brought in to co-create in an ecosystem.

Ecosystem that was created for a large format retailer. The aim was to leverage one another's expertise and insights to help develop a better product, service and a new business model for the company.

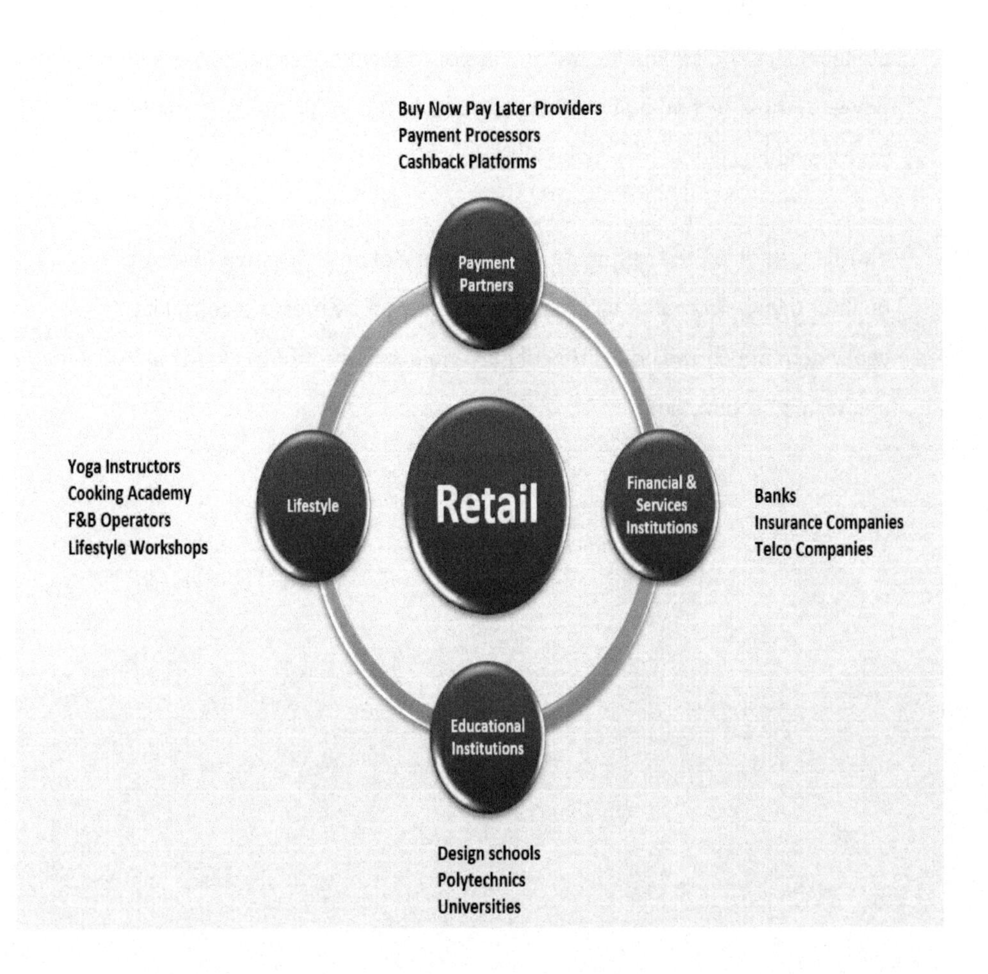

Unilever

Unilever, a global manufacturer of consumer goods with more than a century of experience, offers an extensive selection of products ranging from nourishment and refreshments to personal care essentials. They are dedicated to leveraging their worldwide presence to create beneficial changes across the globe.

Since its founding in the 1920s, Unilever has played a key gatekeeper role in bringing products to consumers by controlling distribution through its brick-and-mortar retail partners. When a small, up-and-coming brand wanted to sit on the shelves of a Walmart or Target, it would typically sell itself to Unilever or one of its competitors, who could utilise its deep relationships to expand distribution and grow the brand.

Unilever greatly exemplifies a company that has embraced digital transformation and the co-creation concept. Unilever has always recognised the value of open innovation in keeping up with a fiercely competitive and global market by partnering with external parties like startups, academics, and individual inventors. Its research and development (R&D) initiatives were among the first to incorporate this concept.

According to a case study conducted by Lancaster University in 2010, Unilever believed that 'access [to innovation] is the new ownership'. This was because they understood that not all great ideas pertaining to Unilever brands would necessarily come from within, despite having €1 billion allocated to R&D spend annually along with an R&D staff strength of 6,200. By eliminating their siloed approach through open innovation, collaboration efforts across various brands together with outside partners became possible for Unilever.

Unilever announced in 2014, the launch of The Unilever Foundry, an open innovation platform that will provide a single entry-point for innovative start-ups seeking to partner with Unilever. Startups are drawn to The Foundry because it offers three key advantages: guidance on marketing, monetary incentives for startups whose concepts tackle Unilever's posted briefs, and entry into Unilever Ventures – the firm's investment arm. By engaging this method, early-stage businesses gain an opportunity to collaborate with a major corporation such as Unilever while enabling the latter to stay up to date with emerging technological advancements. Some of the Unilever's most important innovations have been developed through the Open Innovation model. Its Foundry website, (https://www.theunileverfoundry.com/), shows that it has conducted over 400 pilot projects, invested $50 million and profiled over 40,000 startups.

An example of Unilever Open Innovation in action is the company's Pureit range of water purifying products which was developed in collaboration with a range of technology partners and scientific and public health institutions. Pureit has now been rolled out to all states in India, bringing safe drinking water to people. The device has also been launched in Mexico, Brazil, Indonesia, Bangladesh, and other countries facing a shortage of affordable clean water.

Unilever's Open Innovation platform has a valuable advantage of keeping the company at the forefront. As technological advancements continue to progress quickly, it can be challenging for any organisation to remain current. By collaborating with customers and stakeholders, Unilever gains access to unique ideas and innovations that they may have overlooked on their own. This contributes to outperforming competitors while advancing growth and development.

This platform offers Unilever a great advantage by facilitating the development of more intimate connections with their customers and stakeholders. By closely collaborating with clients, they can gain better insights into their interests and requirements. This fosters customised experiences that boost trust and loyalty in return.

How exactly does Unilever's Open Innovation platform work? There are a few key steps that Unilever takes to make the platform a success.

Encourage participation – Unilever encourages participation by making their platform easy to use and accessible to anyone. They also offer incentives, such as cash prizes to encourage people and companies to submit their ideas.

Evaluate and select ideas – After receiving the ideas, Unilever assesses their potential and chooses the most promising ones. Subsequently, they reach out to the creators of these ideas and work together to actualise them in a collaborative effort.

Collaborate and co-create – Unilever collaborates with innovators to jointly develop novel products, services or experiences while maintaining friendly relations. This collaborative effort includes creating prototypes, conducting tests, and seeking customer feedback for enhancing the idea further.

Launch and commercialise – After confirming the validity of their product or service, Unilever introduces it to customers, creating a buzz and generating excitement. This approach fosters friendliness towards the brand.

Unilever's Open Innovation platform significantly demonstrates how businesses can establish an ecosystem and integrate co-creation as an integral component of their digital transformation strategy. Through collaborative efforts with consumers and other stakeholders, Unilever has been able to design products and services that are better attuned to market demands, while keeping pace with competitors in the industry.

In addition, this approach enables companies to cultivate robust connections with customers through interactive engagement, which ultimately facilitates business success amidst the dynamic contemporary environment.

'We strive to be at the forefront of marketing and media innovation; to have our brands engage in the most creative, efficient and effective ways with the people we serve. Although we have been working with start-ups for years, we now want to scale up our efforts and, ultimately, embed this as a way of working throughout our organisation'.

- Keith Weed, Unilever Chief Marketing and Communications Officer

'The Unilever Foundry will be our single our platform to harness, nurture and evolve thousands of innovative ideas from the entrepreneurial community. It will simplify the way in which small start-ups and entrepreneurs engage with a company of our size, offering an exciting opportunity for the best and brightest to pilot their technology with us. 'Through The Unilever Foundry, we continue the Crafting Brands for Life journey to make our brands more human and more purposeful, while also empowering our marketers to pioneer the future'.

- Marc Mathieu, Senior Vice President, Global Marketing

Johnson & Johnson

Let us examine how Johnson & Johnson, a major player in the healthcare industry, has been teaming up with start-ups to foster creativity and enhance medical care for patients. It is worth noting that Johnson & Johnson has established an extensive track record of partnering with small enterprises for many years now. Their objective, however, remains constant – discovering fresh and inventive approaches that can bring about positive changes in individuals' lives.

One way that Johnson & Johnson has been doing this is through its JLABS incubator programme which offers a range of resources and expert guidance to help small enterprises bring their ideas to fruition. With access to laboratory space, equipment, mentorship and funding opportunities, startups are provided with everything they need for success.

At only 26 years old, Melinda Ritcher found herself on her deathbed after being bitten by a toxic insect while working in Beijing. Despite being a rising star in the tech industry, she decided to focus her efforts on something more meaningful if she survived. After recovering from this life-threatening experience, Richter used her company, Prescience International as a testing ground for JLABS – an idea that had been taking shape during her illness. She envisioned creating a model where start-ups could have access to resources like those offered at larger companies such as dry and wet laboratories along with dedicated operations teams handling administrative tasks.

Ritcher's next move involved collaborating with a healthcare partner to expand the incubator's reach into fresh territories. This led her to join forces with Johnson & Johnson, an innovator that has been setting benchmarks since its inception in 1887 by producing sterilised sutures. Recognising the immense scope for growth across their organisation and worldwide, Johnson & Johnson grasped this opening eagerly.

They were fully aware of how crucial it was to collaborate with fledgling innovators who had first-hand experience as either physicians on the frontline of patient care or business owners themselves, making them familiar with both urgency and necessity.

After two years of fine-tuning, JLABS was born in January 2012, with Richter at the helm.

> **'Through JLABS, we set out to foster innovation across the global life sciences community and help accelerate the development of breakthrough solutions for patients and consumers. Today, JLABS is an integral part of our innovation strategy because we know that a great idea can come from anywhere in the world.'**
>
> — Johnson & Johnson's Chief Scientific Officer Paul Stoffels M.D.

JLABS has produced several success stories, and Arcturus is one of them. The company managed to reduce gene activity in cells infected with Hepatitis B virus by delivering RNA medicine. The co-founders of the company left their jobs and joined JLABS without any substantial proof that their idea would work but had a vision for what they wanted to achieve through innovation.

The two co-founders were not sure that they would make it when they decided to try for JLABS. They had substantial experience in the field but did not have anything to show in terms of research and was concerned that JLABS would not take them seriously. But JLABS knew the men were on to something, based on their cutting-edge idea and strong track record in the field, and offered them the space and materials to get going, including an office, lab benches, freezer and refrigeration units and specialised equipment, not to mention experienced mentors from Johnson & Johnson.

The investment in Arcturus in September 2013 was proven profitable when, after a mere seven months of hard work at JLABS @ San Diego, the diligent team successfully demonstrated that their technology functioned efficiently through animal studies. This achievement not only generated excitement but also gained recognition from external angel investors who provided a round of funding worth $13 million.

'We get companies that already have critical data in hand, but we also have others who have a promising approach, and we see this as a test bed for new ideas. What JLABS does is allow them to generate that proof of concept data that can enable you to get an investment. It's kind of like a chicken and the egg situation: You need the data to get the investment, but you need the investment to get the data. We help start-ups break that cycle.'

— Kara Bortone, who lead the recruitment and selection process at JLABS

In addition to JLABS, Johnson & Johnson has been collaborating with startups and small businesses to jointly create and innovate new solutions. These include joint research and development ventures as well as partnerships that enable the launch of innovative products.

A good example of this is the partnership between Johnson & Johnson and Veracyte, a startup committed to creating innovative cancer diagnostic tools. Together, they have successfully developed an advanced test that can assist doctors in accurately diagnosing specific types of cancer. This characterises how collaborative efforts can result in ground-breaking solutions with significant benefits for patients.

Johnson & Johnson places great importance on partnering with start-ups to advance innovation and enhance the well-being of patients. JLABS, as well as direct collaborations with emerging companies, provides a platform for Johnson & Johnson to access novel concepts and knowledge that have led to pioneering solutions making meaningful contributions to society. This commitment extends beyond conventional diagnostic tools or treatments, but also to developing digital health applications aimed at shaping the future of healthcare through co-creation initiatives.

'We are thrilled to team up with Johnson & Johnson and their Lung Cancer Initiative in the fight against lung cancer,' said Bonnie Anderson, chairman and chief executive officer of Veracyte. 'This strategic collaboration further advances Veracyte's pioneering position in lung cancer diagnosis and underscores the promise of our field of injury science and approach. With the acceleration of our product pipeline, we believe this collaboration expands our addressable lung cancer diagnostic market to a $30 billion to $40 billion global opportunity.

— Bonnie Anderson, chairman and chief executive officer of Veracyte

Johnson & Johnson's Commitment to Innovation:

We know that a great idea can come from anywhere and that it takes partnership to turn ideas into breakthroughs. By connecting the best science and technology entrepreneurs to our global, resources and expertise, we are proud to take on the world's toughest healthcare challenges and aim to improve the health of everyone, everywhere.

Our global innovation partnering teams are here to provide early-stage startups and life science innovators with a single point of entry to Johnson & Johnson. We connect potential collaborators to world-leading resources and aim to support them to advance transformation science and technology across the spectrum of pharmaceutical, medical device and consumer healthcare. We aim to make it easy for collaborators to connect with us, all over the globe.

We operate in every region of the world, with hubs in Boston, London, South San Francisco and Shanghai. Wherever you are in the world, we're excited to connect.

09

Strategy

In this chapter we will be talking about the importance of strategy in business. We will also look at the difference between strategic priorities, objectives and how they are often misunderstood as a strategy.

Strategic priorities are an essential aspect of any business, as they define the key areas that require focus to achieve long-term goals and objectives. The identification of strategic priorities provides a clear direction for decision-making processes and resource allocation within the organisation. These priorities may vary from company to company, depending on their industry, size, and competitive landscape. It is meant to be a long-term plan that provides a consistent direction for the company. I have seen on many occasions where strategic priorities are misunderstood as 'strategy'.

A strategy encompasses the overall blueprint that a company will follow to attain its strategic goals or business targets. It is crucial to understand that a strategy is not merely a set of objectives or aims; rather, it involves analysing how the objectives can be accomplished and detailing the particular measures and strategies that must be implemented for success.

Now, let us discuss why strategic priorities are often misunderstood as a strategy. One of the most basic reasons is because creating a strategy is actually hard work. Most people find this a complicated exercise and, more often than not, adopt the company's objectives and strategic priorities as their strategy. Take the simple example of a person having the objective of becoming healthier, losing weight and gaining well defined abs (or a six-pack!). To achieve this, the person needs a strategy: start exercising (what type of exercises, how often), eat healthily (what to eat, when to eat, how much to eat), get enough sleep, etc. etc. As you can see, whilst the goal and objective may be somewhat easy to define, the strategy to achieve the goal requires a lot more thinking and planning. Often, this also means a lot of research, discussion and planning.

Creating a strategy is hard work for several reasons, including the following:

Complexity of the Business Environment – The contemporary commercial world is intricate and dynamic, posing a challenge to devising an adaptable approach that can react to emerging prospects and obstacles. Companies must manoeuvre various aspects such as rivalry, technological breakthroughs, customer inclinations, financial fluctuations, and alterations in regulations – all capable of influencing their plan.

Uncertainty – The business world is always unpredictable which can pose a problem to formulating an adaptable and successful strategy. Foreseeing upcoming shifts and trends is necessary for businesses, but having absolute certainty about the future remains impossible.

Resource Constraints – Crafting a plan typically demands substantial investment in terms of time, energy, and funds. Companies must allocate resources to conducting research and analysis, engaging with stakeholders, as well as strategising for the future, an undertaking that can weigh heavily on smaller enterprises.

Complexity of Stakeholder Engagement – A successful strategy requires input and buy-in from multiple stakeholders, including employees, customers, investors, and partners. Engaging these stakeholders can be challenging, as they may have different perspectives and priorities.

Execution Challenges – Coming up with a plan is merely the beginning phase. It is equally important for businesses to implement the strategy efficiently by ensuring coherence throughout the organisation and effective leadership, coordination, and communication.

However, by putting in the effort to develop a sound strategy, businesses can improve their competitiveness, respond to new opportunities and challenges, and achieve their goals. So, how do you create a set of strategies to achieve the goals/strategic priorities? There are many ways to do this, but I found that the following three steps will give you a strong foundation to building a good strategy.

(The book Good Strategy, Bad Strategy by Richard Rumelt gave me a good understanding on the topic and has been extremely useful to me in creating strategies for a business. The steps below are from the book. I would recommend reading this book if you are involved in creating strategies for your company).

A Diagnosis – Start with identifying the challenges the business faces in achieving the objective. A diagnosis defines or explains the nature of the challenge. A good diagnosis simplifies the often-overwhelming complexity of reality by identifying certain aspect of the situation as critical.

A Guiding Policy – Once the challenges have been identified and there is an understanding of the challenges, a guiding policy is created to deal with them. This is an overall approach to cope with or overcome the challenges identified.

An Action Plan – A set of coherent actions is then designed to carry out the guiding policy. These are steps that are coordinated with one another to work together in accomplishing the guiding policy.

Sometimes, businesses stop at the guiding policy stage and confuse this as having defined a strategy. Strategy is about doing something. To complete the work of defining a strategy, it must contain action. Ensuring that the actions are coordinated and built upon one another will help in defining a good and clear strategy.

However, it is key to understand that these three steps are the main concepts around defining a strategy and are the start to formulating a full strategy. There are other factors that need to be included to form a strategy, such as vision, hierarchy of goals and objectives, references to time span and scope, and ideas about adaptation and change. Basically, strategy is all about using your strengths to overcome weaknesses or to seize the best opportunities. Nowadays, experts talk a lot about potential advantages like being first to market, having size and scope on your side, benefiting from network effects or a great reputation. All of these can be important in their own way, but they overlook two crucial strengths.

Coherent strategy – A well-coordinated plan that aligns policies and actions is crucial for success. A proficient strategy not only leverages current strengths but also generates more strength by virtue of its cohesive structure. Unfortunately, many businesses tend to overlook this vital aspect and aim for disparate objectives instead or, even worse, contradictory goals.

Different New Outlook – By making subtle adjustments to our perspective, we can unlock new strengths and opportunities. By rethinking the competitive landscape and looking at it from a fresh angle, we may discover completely novel patterns of advantage that were previously hidden. These game-changing insights give rise to some of the most effective strategies imaginable, ones that allow us to achieve unprecedented success.

I recently spent some time consulting for a big format retail organisation on their transformation plan. As part of the transformation work, we had to establish the new strategic priorities / objectives and create a strategy to achieve the objectives. Below is an illustration of the steps that were used to define the strategy. It is a simplified version of the work as the aim is to give you an idea of how to use the three steps to create the strategy. Before creating the strategy, we went through the exercise of identifying where the business is today and where it would like to be in the future, its customers today and in the future, as well as the resources available.

Steps:

Objective – To Provide Seamless & Frictionless Shopping Experience

Challenge (There were many, but I am only highlighting one.) – Low service standards at physical store location.

Guiding policies (There were three guiding policies for the challenge stated above but I am only highlighting one.) – Provide training to raise service standard to best in class

Action Plan – Establish customer service values and minimum service standards, Mystery Shopping evaluation–quarterly, Identify training courses or work with a partner to train staff on service standards

Identify a Champion for each Action Plan and allocate a support team

Set deadlines for continuous review of the progress in executing the Action Plan.

Intuit

Intuit is a financial software company that has been around for over three decades. It was founded in 1983 by Scott Cook and Tom Proulx. Scott Cook, the creator of Intuit and a former employee at Procter & Gamble, recognised that personal computers could replace pen-and-paper accounting. He searched for a programmer to bring his vision to life and ultimately met Tom Proulx while attending Stanford University. The two established Intuit in a small room at University Avenue in Palo Alto.

Intuit began its journey with Quicken, a personal finance software, which gained immense popularity among users. As time passed by, the company broadened its range of products and introduced QuickBooks, an accounting software for small businesses and TurboTax, a tax preparation tool. With these three exceptional products, Intuit solidified its position as one of the leading players in the financial software domain. Quicken's initial version was developed using Microsoft's BASIC programming language for IBM PC and UCSD Pascal for Apple II by Tom Proulx despite facing tough competition from 12 other similar products.

Since then, Intuit has grown into a multinational organisation and has 14,200 employees with 20 offices in nine countries serving millions of customers. At the end of 2022 it had a revenue of $12.7 billion.

However, Intuit's success story is not limited to the development of successful products alone. It is also a testament to their proficiency in adapting and transforming themselves strategically in response to market trends and technological advancements. This reflects the company's commitment to professional growth and evolution over time.

In the late 80s, Intuit made big strides towards success. Quicken had become a popular personal finance application in just a short amount of time and was selling like hotcakes all over the world, competing with well-known software like WordPerfect and Lotus 1-2-3. In three years, its revenue skyrocketed from $20 million to $55 million by 1991 while their team grew significantly – reaching about 425 employees that year alone.

In the 90s, Intuit went through a rough patch. They were getting over their Microsoft merger let down and dealing with issues with software sales. Not many people were buying packaged software because computers already had it installed, and lots of folks who wanted personal finance software already owned Quicken. Plus, the internet was starting to take over which could mean bad news for standalone programmes like theirs. Intuit did not give up and accept defeat. They reinvented themselves as a speedy internet company, aiming to use their brand recognition to attract customers and build trust.

> **'The internet pushed us to adapt quickly and be okay with making mistakes - so long as we learned from them.'**
>
> — Intuit's founder, Scott Cook

Intuit made a big move in 1997 by selling off parts of its business that were not essential. They sold their online banking and electronic transaction processing subsidiary, Intuit Services Corporation, to Checkfree who deals with financial electronic commerce services and products. Additionally, they also got rid of their consumer software and direct marketing operations called Parsons by selling it to Broderbund Software - the makers of video games, educational software, and productivity tools.

In the early 2000s, Intuit underwent a major transformation as it encountered heightened rivalry from online financial services. With numerous individuals turning to the internet for their banking and other financial needs, Intuit recognised the need to evolve to remain relevant in this rapidly changing landscape. To achieve this, Intuit adopted an online approach and rebranded itself as a cloud-based software enterprise. Instead of marketing packaged software directly to customers, the company opted for providing its services via the internet. This was a risky decision. However, it proved to be beneficial in keeping up with ever-evolving market trends whilst also boosting growth potential and maintaining competitiveness.

In 2002, Cook found himself facing a frustrating situation. After meticulously analysing the data from Intuit's 10 years of new product introductions, he discovered that the company was not getting satisfactory returns on its huge investments. This realisation came about because too many products were failing to succeed in the market. Although considered an exceptionally well-managed organisation by traditional standards, Cook attributed this failure rate to an insufficient management paradigm for sustaining innovation in today's world.

Consequently, he had to face a challenging conclusion after his diagnosis of root causes: significant changes needed implementing within both him and his company going forward if they hoped to maintain continuous progress and success.

An example of the change needed was how one of Intuit's flagship products, TurboTax, due to its seasonal sales cycle coinciding with the tax season in the US, had developed an overly cautious approach which stifled experimentation and agility. To overcome this issue, Intuit needed a new policy that would allow for greater flexibility and adaptability.

Consequently, today over 500 different changes are tested during the two-and-a-half months leading up to tax season via running about seventy tests per week. The team can seamlessly deploy these changes on Thursday evening each week and review them by Monday while coming to informed conclusions starting Tuesday before rebuilding newer ones for release the following Thursday night again – a process significantly more streamlined than in previous years!

Another of Intuit's successful strategies was prioritising customer satisfaction. The management recognised the customers' desire for user-friendly financial software accessible on any device and from anywhere. By providing online services, Intuit fulfilled this requirement and sustained its top rank in the financial software sector. Intuit also takes a personal approach to better understand its users, using programmes like 'Follow me Home' to gain insights into their experiences and identify areas for improvement.

By investing 10,000 hours each year in visiting real customers, the company is able to deepen its understanding of customer needs and preferences. These efforts not only enhance existing products but also provide valuable feedback on potential new solutions.

Intuit has always been into trying new stuff, including buying up other companies. They have made some smart purchases over the years that have helped them grow their products and know-how on things like payroll and payment processing. One of their coolest moves was grabbing Mint, a really hip finance app loved by lots of younger folks. By scooping up Mint, Intuit brought loads more people on board with all kinds of awesome money management tools customised just for them.

The purchase of Credit Karma in 2020, a personal finance app that helps consumers manage their credit was another remarkable strategy. Intuit now has a huge group of customers and fresh information from their recent takeovers. They can use this to improve their financial products and services even more.

Intuit's journey shows how crucial it is to adapt and to have a solid game plan in the tech industry. Its strategy of being open to changes and putting customers first, has managed to keep Intuit ahead of the competition and has transformed it into one of the top players in the financial software industry worldwide. Their dedication to fresh ideas and savvy takeovers means they will probably be dominating the tech industry for the foreseeable future.

Although 46 similar products were on the market when Intuit launched Quicken, in 1983, it immediately became the market leader in personal finance software and has held that position for three decades. This is because Quicken was so well designed that using it is intuitive. But by the time Brad Smith became CEO, in 2008, the company had become overly focused on adding incremental features that delivered ease of use but not delight. What was missing was an emotional connection with customers. He and his team set out to integrate design thinking into every part of Intuit.

They changed the layout of the office, reduced the number of cubes, and added more collaboration spaces and places for impromptu work. They increased the number of designers by nearly 600% and now hold quarterly design conferences.

They bring in people who have created exceptionally designed products, such as the Nest thermostat and the Kayak travel website, to share insights with Intuit employees. The company acquired one start-up, called Mint, and collaborates with another, called ZenPayroll, to improve customer experience.

Implementing a Digital Transformation Strategy

In today's digital era, it has become absolutely essential for any business to have a digital transformation strategy in place. However, executing the strategy can often be quite challenging, just like with any other strategic initiative. That said, there are several steps that businesses can take to ensure their digital transformation strategy is effectively implemented. It is like building a house; you need to start by laying a strong foundation and then add layer upon layer to create a solid structure. The same goes for digital transformation. First, you would need to identify the key elements and then slowly build upon them so that you have a sustainable, successful digital strategy. Here are some tips to help you get started.

Step 1 – Start with your people. It is imperative to ensure that there is a sold leadership team in place. As you would have gathered from Chapter 6 (People at the Centre of Transformation), ensuring that you have the right skill set, mindset and culture is vital for any transformation project. With the right leadership team in place, they will be able to guide the organisation in developing a solid transformation strategy.

Step 2 – Define Your Goals and Objectives. The next step is to define a set of goals and objectives for what the business is trying to achieve through the transformation. Answering questions such as the ones below will guide you in defining the goals and objectives.

- Where do we want to be?
- Where are we now?
- How are we going to get there?
- What challenges are we looking to solve?
- How will we measure success?

Step 3 – Assess Your Current State. Once the goals and objectives have been set, pay attention to your current state of business. What are the current processes in place? Is the technology currently being used in the business sufficient to achieve the goals and objectives? Do we have the right skill sets in the organisation? This evaluation will assist you in identifying necessary modifications and provide a starting point for monitoring your advancement.

Step 4 – Develop a Strategy. After you have clearly understood the goals and objectives and evaluated the current situation, it is time to devise a strategy. The plan must be comprehensive and outline in as much detail as possible how the business will reach its targets, which technological resources should come into play, what procedural modifications are necessary, etc. In addition to these, resource limitations, budgetary considerations and how success will be measured should also shape your strategy. The 'Diagnosis, Guiding Policy and Action Plan' concept should serve as a guidepost throughout this process.

Step 5 – Implement the Strategy. Once the strategy has been established, the execution phase starts. This may involve upgrading your technology, changing your processes, or training your employees. This is where many organisations struggle. Whilst it is hard work to create a good strategy, it is even harder to execute it! Take the example of changing the mindset of the organisation to be more agile as one part of the strategy. The actual process of changing the mindset takes a lot of work, time, and patience. Changing the mindset of people is one of the most difficult things to achieve. Therefore, it is really important to have a solid plan for implementation and assembling a team that can handle the whole process. Trust me, it will save you some serious headaches in the long run.

Step 6 – Measure and Adapt. The final step in any transformation is to measure the progress and adapt as needed. This involves keeping a record of your advancements against your goals and objectives and making alterations as necessary. It is also important to constantly reassess your strategy, and to make changes as per the evolution of your business. Remember that the strategy is a roadmap and is not cast in stone. Being agile to be able to adapt to changes is crucial.

As the business world continues to evolve, it is crucial for companies to keep up with technological advancements to remain competitive. This is why implementing a digital transformation strategy should be at the top of every organisation's priority list. By following these steps outlined above and taking an innovative approach towards change, you can help your company thrive in today's ever-changing landscape.

Contribution by Christophe Bacon, Founder & Managing Director at Omnistrada

A PRAGMATIC APPROACH TO DIGITAL TRANSFORMATION for SMEs

For most businesses, COVID-19 drastically exposed the weakness of their digital capability, or the lack thereof. The other few forward-thinking businesses, that have continuously invested in digital transformation programmes prior to the crisis, are now better positioned to: leverage their tech-stack and digital capabilities; adapt to changes in customer needs and expectations; adjust their value chain; be agile; gain market share; and explore new operational models and marketing tactics.

The pandemic has changed the business landscape, with digital channels often becoming the primary, and sometimes sole, customer-engagement model, and automated processes becoming a primary driver for productivity across departments.

These structural changes are here to stay.

Business leaders who wish to close the growing digital divide between category leaders and laggards must start with a commitment to making digital transformation an essential part of the organisation's growth model and future success. It cannot be left to be a vague hope, or a fall-back option triggered by COVID-19.

This means embedding digital capabilities at the core of their objectives, orienting, and organising resources accordingly, and holding business leaders and their teams accountable for results.

Whilst many non-business-critical programmes have been postponed, the crisis has showcased the value of digital transformation initiatives. The consensus is that growth-led transformation programmes need to swiftly start or resume. Businesses need to reassess their digital capabilities and accelerate their transformation programmes, not only to survive and provide short-term solutions to employees, customers, and stakeholders, but also to position the business for the long term.

Fundamentally, digital transformation is not just about technology. It is a transformative journey that enables businesses to become truly customer-centric, omnichannel and personalised, and can only be successful if the entire organisation works towards a common goal. To be successful, companies need to enable the business to continually evolve and adapt to changes in customer needs and expectations. Digital transformation experts agree that the key factors for success are leadership commitment, capability building, change management, technology upgrades, and communication.

Ultimately, successful implementations require companies to articulate a common vision and clear objectives, a realistic business plan, a precise scope of work, and the necessary resource and project plan that addresses all aspects of the omnichannel business stack.

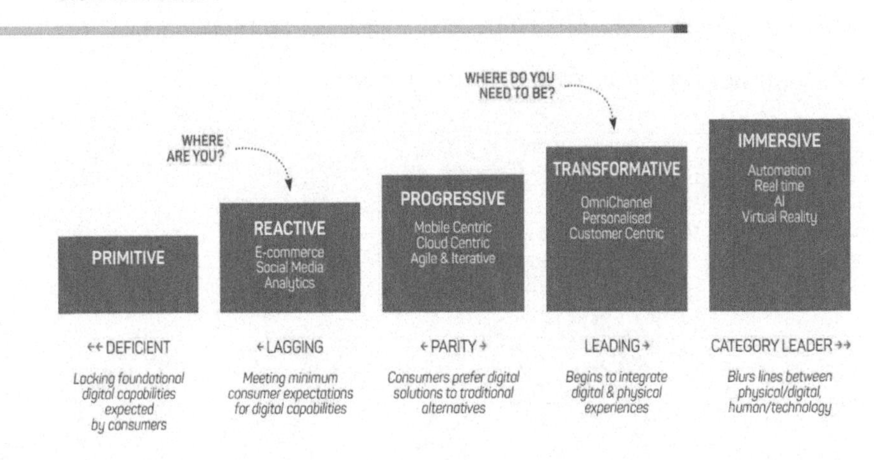

Customer journeys are not linear but consist of a series of interactions between traditional and digital channels and can vary significantly by customer segment. To design an omnichannel journey, companies must gain detailed visibility into their customer personas. Only then can they design end-to-end omnichannel signature experiences, that integrate human experiences (interactions with individuals, employees, and social groups), with physical ones (products, objects, stores, settings that can be experienced) and digital ones (digital touchpoints, technology solutions, automation and personalisation), and that provide a seamless omnichannel customer journey.

Only digital transformations that are omnichannel allow businesses to address complex customer journeys, provide unique and memorable signature experiences across touchpoints, and increase customer satisfaction.

SIGNATURE OMNICHANNEL EXPERIENCES

TRULY REMARKABLE SIGNATURE OMNICHANNEL EXPERIENCES ARE DELIBERATELY ENGINEERED TO BE:

Engineered, tested and executed with prescriptive methods to achieve levels of consistency across the organisation

Creating lasting memories with experiences that engage all five senses: sight, hearing, smell, taste and touch

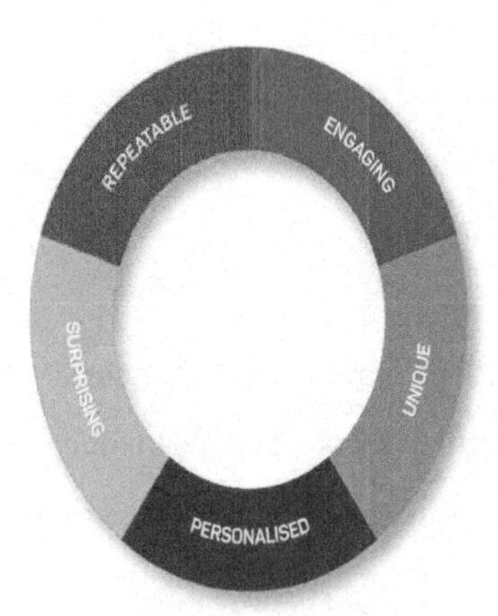

Incorporating unexpected and delightful interactions into the experiences

Including methods and language unique to the brand that are surprising and authentic

Making customers feel valued and that the experience was just created for them

To elaborate, an actionable omnichannel transformation strategy, businesses must make sure that it addresses customer expectations and focuses on future value propositions, identifying industry and customer trends, as well as potential value shifts driven by disruption and new players. Benchmarking the company's value proposition against category leaders and emerging winners from the crisis – including in other industries, and understanding the positioning and capabilities of potential partners and competitors, will help assess the validity and feasibility of the envisioned initiatives. It is then important to review and analyse the possible impact and expected value creation across the value chain and business models. This will reveal potential capability gaps, in people, expertise and solutions, and highlight new competency requirements.

The leadership team then needs to articulate a detailed plan and roadmap, with clearly identified milestones and targets for the organisation to aim for, precise scopes of work and necessary resource planning. In the strategic planning phase, we recommend companies to initially identify easy targets with low-hanging fruits to help build momentum toward broader, more ambitious digital transformation goals. Targeting short-term and practical goals will allow the business to test and learn, whilst having a positive impact on customers' experience, helping improve customer satisfaction and boosting sales in the early stage of the transformation.

The strategic plan and roadmap must be communicated clearly to all stakeholders, to share the organisation's priorities, manage expectations about the transformation and secure buy-in from the entire organisation. Launching a digital transformation effort often seems like a daunting task and many businesses are overwhelmed by the idea of having to revamp their entire technology stack and digital approach. Focusing on the customer, the right strategic planning and Agile methods are the first steps of your digital transformation. Such an approach will help you build a roadmap to help you gain market share and stand out from the competition, and to remain relevant to your customers.

BUILDING STONES OF A SUCCESSFUL DIGITAL TRANSFORMATION

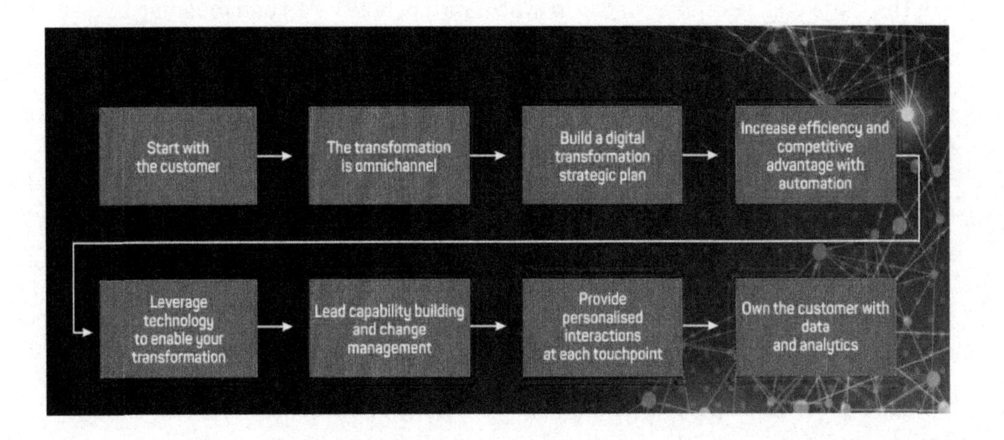

10

New Business Model

This chapter focuses on highlighting the importance of discovering a new business model as part of the digital transformation strategy. It is an undeniable fact that technology has revolutionised every aspect of our lives and continues to evolve at breakneck speed. This evolution presents immense potential for businesses to prosper in unexplored territories. However, tapping into these possibilities demands adapting and executing a well-planned digital transformation strategy equipped with new-age business models tailored for success in today's world.

Why is finding a new business model so important in the digital transformation strategy? A business model is essentially how a company makes money. And in today's fast-paced, technology-driven world, it is important for businesses to constantly evaluate and potentially change their business models to stay ahead of the competition and continue to deliver value to customers. Adding new sources of revenue or evolving the core business to ensure that it stays relevant in the current (and foreseeable future) landscape can be very beneficial to a business.

Remember the story of Netflix? Over time, Netflix reinvented its corporate plan and switched to a subscription-based business model where users could lease a DVD at a fixed monthly fee. At the very peak of their DVD business, Netflix decided to rebrand again and shifted to online streaming. This emerging market allowed them to expand globally.

The retail industry is a great example of why businesses need to transform and find new business models. It was not that long ago that physical retail stores were the only choice for anyone wanting to go shopping be it for necessities or for a leisurely shopping spree. In the current environment we live in, especially due to the pandemic, things have changed dramatically. In 2023, it is estimated that 33.3% of the world's population will be online shoppers, a 3.1% year-over-year increase from 2022.

E-commerce is a formidable force and has completely changed how retail businesses operate. Amazon, for example, not only disrupted how people shop but is dominating the retail industry in many ways. The rise of other marketplaces such as Lazada and Shopee in Asia, Alibaba in China, Flipkart in India are all examples of how the retail industry has changed. This, however, does not mean that the brick-and-mortar stores are no longer relevant or will be extinct.

They still play an essential role in our society today. However, what is clear is that they need to adapt and evolve by embracing technology and integrating e-commerce into their operations if they want to remain competitive.

This does not just apply to the retail industry. Almost every other industry is being disrupted by technology. Technology creates new challenges but also presents new opportunities. It is, therefore, vital that businesses keep innovating and looking for new business models to drive their evolution. You may be familiar with the statement, **'Past performance is no indicator of future returns'**, which can be found in most investment brochures or advertisements. This statement should be applied to all businesses! Just because the business has been successful in the past, does not mean that it is guaranteed that it will be successful in the future. If it fails to evolve, there is a high possibility that it will become irrelevant. This is like a ship trying to sail against the wind – it needs to continually adjust its sails to navigate the waves while still moving forward. If it fails to do so, it will likely crash into rocks or be tossed backwards into the current.

How do you evolve into a new business model? There is no one specific set of rules or steps to follow but some key points to consider are as follows:

Spend time understanding your customers and the market that you are competing in. This insight will give you a better understanding of what your customer likes and does not like. It is data, which you can then use to come up with new products or services that are relevant to them and meet their needs.

Think about how you can leverage technology to deliver these new products or services. For instance, you could use data and analytics to better understand your customers and personalise your offerings to meet their individual needs (Example: the use of Customer Data Platforms for predictive analytics and personalisation).

The concept of experimentation and innovation that we covered in Chapter 3 plays a key part in ensuring that your workforce is constantly looking at new and innovative ideas. The importance of people and mindset which we have covered is a vital ingredient as well.

Think about what your customers want right now compared to before. Consider who else could benefit from what you are offering and think of other ways you could use your resources to provide better services. Ask yourself, 'What if?' when thinking about changing up how you run your business. It is a powerful question.

Be in the know. Read industry reports and research trends, be curious about what technologies are being developed and how your business could possibly leverage the technology. Get into networking sessions with industry peers but also with other industry players. You would then get a better and wider perspective of what is being developed. For example, going to start up conferences could open possibilities of collaboration that could differentiate you from the competition.

In summary, operating in today's rapidly evolving digital age, the importance of discovering a new business model cannot be overstated. To remain competitive and satisfy customer demands, it is imperative for enterprises to continuously adapt and adjust their approach as needed. Through thorough market analysis, leveraging technology to innovate new offerings, and with the right culture, organisations can successfully discover an innovative business model that propels them towards success.

Motorola

Brothers, Paul and Joseph Galvin, established the Galvin Manufacturing Corporation in Chicago back in 1928. The company's initial product was a gadget called the 'battery eliminator' which allowed direct-current, battery-powered radios to connect to alternating current that was commonly used in over 60 per cent of U.S. households at that time. In 1930, they launched an affordable car radio named Motorola, which soon became the top choice for new cars as well as aftermarket kits. Later, they ventured into producing tabletop radios for homes and introduced their push-button dialling feature through its car radio offering by 1937.

In the year 1977, Motorola created a portable wireless phone that could connect to public telephone networks by utilising short-range 'cells'. Cellular systems were being installed in most major cities globally by 1985. In the year 1989, the company released the MicroTAC flip cell phone which became popular worldwide as both an essential means of communication and a status symbol. The company dominated the mobile phone market for a long time and came up with lots of cool stuff, like releasing the first-ever cell phone regular people could buy – the DynaTAC 8000X – back in '83.

The Motorola Razr, introduced in the early 2000s, proved to be a massive hit with global sales reaching an impressive 120 million units. The initial success of this phone allowed Motorola to maintain its position as a successful company. However, over time, things took a downturn for the brand. Between 2007 and 2009 alone, it incurred losses amounting to $4.3 billion. Motorola went downhill quickly because smartphones became a big thing in the early 2000s. Apple and Samsung came out with their own versions, which totally changed the game.

Even though Motorola was already ahead of everyone else back then, they still found it tough to keep up with these new types of phones. Back in October 2009, Motorola came out with the Droid, their very own smartphone meant to give iPhone a run for its money. It did okay at first, but when compared to the fresh batch of smartphones coming into the market, it just could not keep up. Brands like Samsung and LG had a better idea about what customers were really after and Apple kept releasing new versions of their phone which were much better.

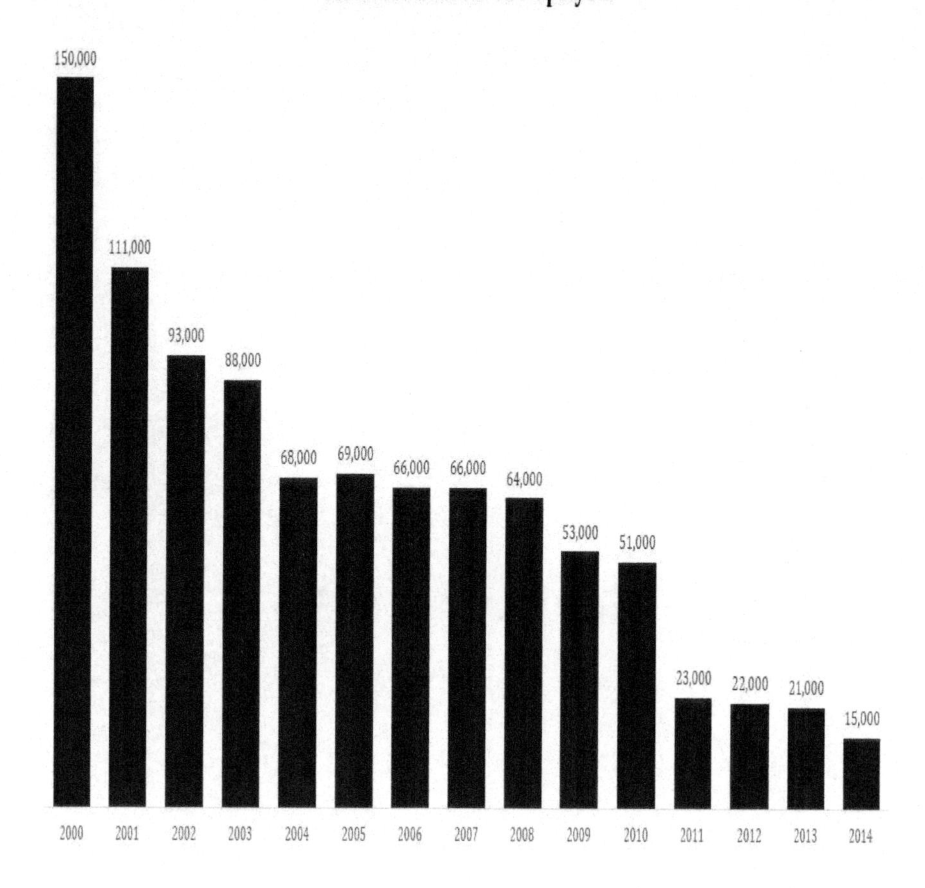
Motorola Number of Employees
150,000
111,000
93,000
88,000
68,000
69,000
66,000
66,000
64,000
53,000
51,000
23,000
22,000
21,000
15,000
2000
2001
2002
2003
2004
2005
2006
2007
2008
2009
2010
2011
2012
2013
2014

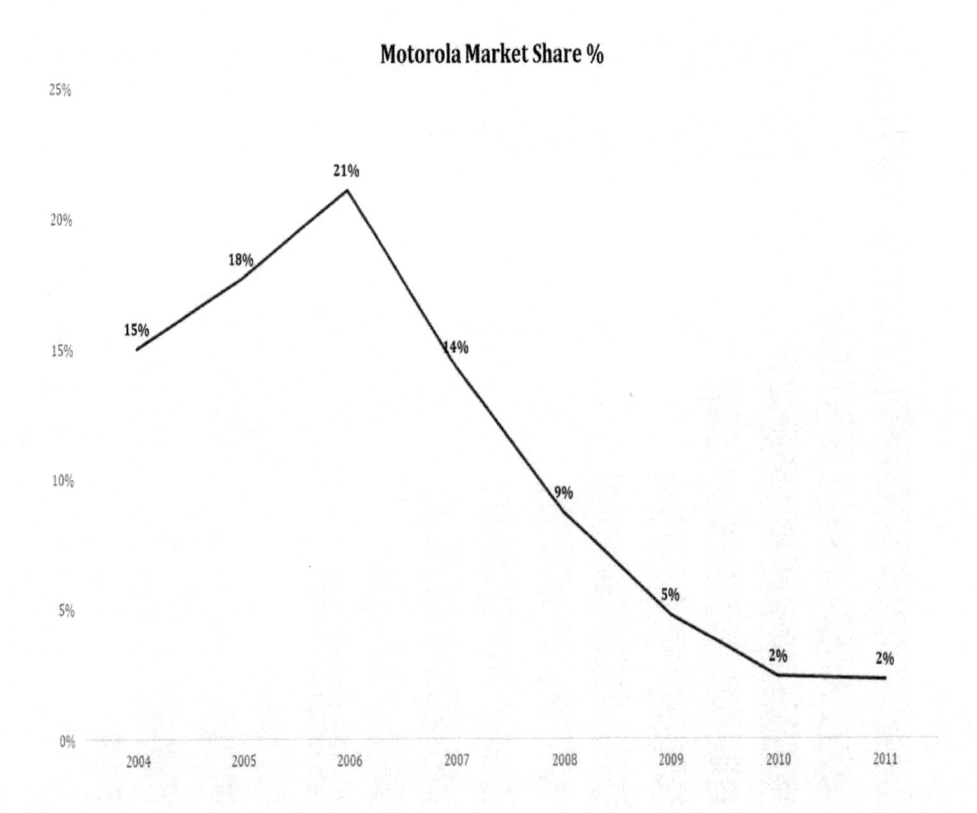
Motorola Market Share %
25%
20%
15%
10%
5%
0%
21%
18%
15%
14%
9%
5%
2%
2%
2004
2005
2006
2007
2008
2009
2010
2011

Motorola's decline can be attributed to their failure to adapt and evolve into a new business model. Despite investing vast amounts in research and development, Motorola failed to capitalise on technology that could have propelled them towards a more innovative future. They remained focused on producing mobile phones instead of understanding consumers pain points and innovating to solve those problems which was what the smartphones did! In essence, while smartphones revolutionised the industry by providing users with access to countless features and addressing pain points experienced by many consumers, Motorola failed miserably at recognising this change.

This lack of innovation ultimately led them down the path of irrelevance in an increasingly competitive market dominated by smartphone giants such as Apple and Samsung. Besides, Motorola's gadgets were frequently perceived as not being as inventive when compared with its rivals and the organisation found it difficult to keep up with the quick advancement of the mobile phone industry.

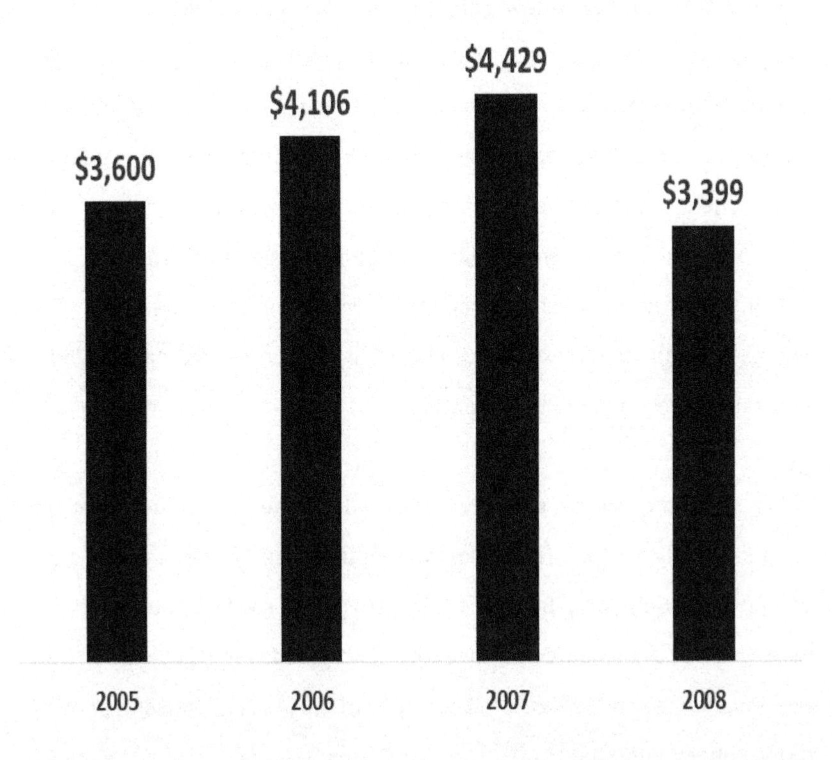

Despite large investments being made in R&D, the failure to leverage it and evolve to a new business model was detrimental to Motorola.

Another reason for Motorola's decline was the inability to incorporate 3G into their devices. Whilst other industry players recognised the importance of 3G, Motorola did not. U.S. wireless carriers were Motorola's biggest customers, and they thought there was no need for 3G. Complacency and a lack of agility was the key issue. When they did try to jump on the bandwagon, it was too late.

Looking back, another takeaway is that whilst Apple focused all its efforts on making one amazing phone, Motorola was trying to juggle dozens of different models at the same time. Apple also quickly adapted to the shift from hardware to software driving the mobile phone industry and focused on this change which Motorola failed to do. Agility was one of the main problems at Motorola. Motorola's decline in market share compounded the problem. With no new revenue streams and inability to find a new business model, their financials continued to suffer. This in turn made it more difficult for the company to invest in new technology and compete with the new entrants to the market.

Motorola made several attempts to try and recover its position in the industry. It split its business into two: Motorola Mobility and Motorola Solutions. Motorola Mobility continued with its consumer business which made handsets and set-top boxes while Motorola Solutions sold police radios and barcode scanners to government and business customers. In 2012, Google purchased Motorola Mobility, and this was seen as a potential comeback for Motorola due to Google's strength in technology and innovation. This did not turn out as everyone had anticipated. Google's aim was to get its hands on Motorola's 17,000 patents.

The rationale behind it was that owning these patents would help Google protect its Android operating system from infringements. There was also the potential for licensing revenues by pooling patents and leasing them to competitors. in 2014, Google sold Motorola Mobility to Lenovo. Lenovo gave hope that Motorola could be revived as they had a good reputation for innovating but once again, this was false hope.

The company continued to struggle and was unable to effectively compete with the new entrants.

Motorola's demise was due to many factors, but the key points are:

- Lack of innovation
- Inability to transform to a new business model
- Lack of agility to respond to market changes

These led to a significant drop in market share which contributed to a devastating blow to its financials. Despite attempts to recover its position, the company was unable to regain its place as a market leader and was ultimately overtaken by other companies in the market.

For most organisations, change is difficult. Transformation of a business, as we have seen thus far, requires the leaders of the organisation to consider many aspects to initiate change. Some of the key reasons organisations find it hard to change is due to what we call success traps. It is easy for organisations to get caught in success traps such as competency, talent, and metrics. These traps hinder their transformation.

Competency trap – A competency trap is that false belief that your past principles, ideas and mental models will continually lead to future successes and better judgment. It is a tendency to rely on familiar tools, skills, or routines without measuring their effectiveness now and in the future.

Talent trap – Every organisation wants to nurture and manage the best talent available and obtain value from the expertise of its workforce. However, most organisations focus on hiring for existing roles instead of identifying the profile of talent that might be needed in the future.

Ed Zander, CEO, Motorola, insists that he saw the smartphone onslaught coming but Motorola 'didn't have the DNA or the people' to understand the software involved.

Metrics trap – Every company has their own defined metrics of success (KPIs). These typically measure efficiency, quality, cost, and profitability. Most of these targets focus the management team on short-term performance and ROIs. There is nothing inherently wrong with this as it is important for the business to perform in the short term to keep growing and to ensure that there is sufficient liquidity in the business. However, with the lack of long-term thinking, it usually means no one in the organisation is focusing on experimentation and innovation – and we have seen how this affected Motorola.

'It usually takes nine to 15 months to design a phone and get it to stores. But what Motorola needs, he added, is not just a good-looking handset but a whole new series with a good selling point or theme. This may take two to three years to develop. Motorola may come up with a new innovative design language, but that is no longer a sufficient competitive differentiator. You need that plus a new consumer value proposition'.

— Yankee Group analyst John Jackson

11

Constant Re-invention

As we saw in the previous chapter with Motorola, being complacent can lead to a disastrous outcome for a business. If your business is competing in a very competitive market, it is possible that your competitor may be working on an innovation that could seriously harm your business. If your organisation currently enjoys huge share of the market that you are operating in, maintaining status quo with no innovation is also asking for trouble as it only takes a new entrant or even a small start up to disrupt the industry that you are in (remember the Blockbuster and Netflix story in Chapter 2).

In the constantly evolving environment that we live in, it is extremely important that companies understand that transformation strategies are never completed. It is an ever-evolving process and keeping a constant eye on the future is a fundamental element for any organisation to stay relevant and successful. Businesses must keep pace with changes to remain relevant and competitive.

Technological changes – As we have seen over the years, new technologies keep popping up and the rate at which new technologies are being developed is much faster than in the past. If companies do not keep up with the times, they will fall behind. To stay current, businesses need to be open to trying out and implementing new technology into their day-to-day operations.

Customer expectations – It is crucial for businesses to consider the evolving demands and desires of their customers to remain competitive and successful. Therefore, it is imperative that companies have a comprehensive understanding of the requirements of their target audience to adeptly respond and modify their strategies accordingly. To achieve this objective, organisations must stay abreast of consumer trends and behaviour patterns whilst ensuring prompt response rates to any alterations within the market dynamics.

Competition – In today's business world, keeping up with the constantly evolving landscape is crucial. The competition has become more intense than ever before and there is a risk of being left behind if one does not adapt quickly. To stay ahead in a cut-throat market, businesses must be proactive in continuously reinventing themselves and enhancing their operations and processes to remain at the top.

How can a business ensure that it is constantly innovating and reinventing itself? All the topics we have covered so far in this book are essential in doing so, but let me summarise a few crucial areas:

Strategy – Having clearly defined goals or objectives on where the company wants to go backed by a detailed strategy on how the goals and objectives will be met is crucial. This will enable everyone in the organisation to be on the same page working on the same objectives.

Leadership – A crucial element is to have competent leadership in place. It is essential for organisations to have leaders who recognise the significance of continuous innovation and are dedicated to instigating change. These leaders should possess the capability of establishing a well-defined perspective for their company's future and proficiently convey that vision with staff, clients, and other stakeholders.

Technology – One important element in the continual process of improvement involves utilising technology. To remain competitive, businesses must skilfully incorporate technology to initiate change and maintain a cutting-edge approach. This requires comprehensive knowledge of current technological advancements and effective implementation that satisfies both business objectives and customer requirements.

Culture – Besides effective leadership, it is imperative for companies to establish a culture that promotes innovation. This involves creating an atmosphere where employees are encouraged and empowered to propose novel ideas while the company displays a willingness to take risks and explore uncharted territory. Cultivating such an innovative culture is indispensable for achieving successful transformation as it allows organisations to perpetually enhance their operations to keep pace with changing times.

Customer focused – Placing your customers' requirements as top priority implies that you are prioritising them in your business strategy. This technique is referred to as customer-centricity, which necessitates comprehending their discomfort points, wants and choices. By doing this, you can design goods and services that fulfil their needs resulting in increased contentment and loyalty of clients. To foster innovation, it is crucial to comprehend the requirements and anticipations of your customers. This knowledge can help you envision their upcoming needs and wants, enabling you to invent novel products and services that cater to those demands ahead of others in the market.

In addition, refining your current offerings based on customer feedback not only helps enhance them but also allows for continuous advancement which will keep you a step ahead of competitors. Having knowledge about the needs and behaviour of your customers can provide you with a competitive edge. This allows you to discover opportunities in the market that are unfulfilled and develop products or services to fill those gaps, distinguishing yourself from competitors. Additionally, delivering exceptional customer service helps you stand out among many options available which could lead to attracting new clients while retaining existing ones.

To sum up, the key to achieving success in today's swiftly evolving business environment is constant innovation. To stay competitive and relevant, organisations must possess a distinct future outlook, effective leadership abilities and a culture of creativity. In addition, emphasis must be placed on technology adoption, customer centricity and an unwavering dedication to consistent learning and growth. By consistently innovating, businesses can maintain their position as leaders while thriving amidst dynamic market conditions over time.

Amazon

Amazon's success can be attributed to its continuous innovation, which has allowed it to remain one of the most prosperous companies globally. In recognition that the internet was growing rapidly by 2300% annually in July 5, 1994, Bezos and his then-wife, MacKenzie Scott, left their jobs at D.E. Shaw (a global investment and technology development firm) and began an online bookshop in a rented garage in Bellevue, Washington. This marked the beginning of Amazon's business journey. With almost $250,000 from Bezos' parents as start-up capital, Amazon started operating on July 16,1995 as an online bookseller with a vast collection available for anyone with internet access, to buy from anywhere they are based around the world.

The company has since diversified its operations over time through constant reinvention aimed at remaining relevant and competitive amidst changing business environments. It presently focuses on e-commerce, cloud computing solutions, digital streaming facilities including music videos/audios among others, advertising solutions and artificial intelligence.

Amazon prioritised delivering excellent customer service and refining its operations and procedures right from the start. As time went by, the business diversified to offer a broad selection of items such as electronics, apparel, and even groceries. Nevertheless, Amazon's triumph isn't solely due to its capacity for selling an extensive array of merchandise; it is also credited to its dedication towards constant reimagining. The company has always centred on anticipating future trends and devising novel solutions that cater effectively to customers' requirements.

Amazon regards ideas as valuable assets that are on par with its workforce and equipment. Jeff Bezos employs a pioneering strategy for developing e-commerce, which involves translating opportunities into a flow of concepts that can be executed effectively. The company's innovation approach is centred around meeting the needs of their customers by using data to listen to them attentively. By doing so, Amazon gains insight into what consumers' desire and this knowledge inspires new creations and innovations tailored to their preferences automatically.

Amazon's dedication to technology has played a crucial role in its ability to continually innovate and transform. From the company's inception, Bezos was determined to utilise technology as a means of effecting change and enhancing the customer experience. Amazon has been at the forefront of implementing emerging technologies such as robotics for more efficient e-commerce fulfilment operations; artificial intelligence for logistics, warehousing, and distribution purposes.

Alexa-enabled online shopping is another noteworthy addition that provides customers with voice-activated assistance throughout their purchasing journey, allowing them hands-free interaction instead of relying on traditional clicking or tapping methods. Additionally, this intelligent assistant can perform various tasks including playing music or checking weather updates by simply communicating with Alexa itself.

Amazon's emphasis on innovation is exemplified by the creation of Amazon Prime, which was introduced in 2005. This subscription service provides customers with complimentary two-day shipping and various other perks such as streaming music and videos. Amazon Prime was a daring and inventive decision that has played a significant role in the company's triumphs throughout time.

Over the years, Jeff Bezos has implemented a philosophy of remaining firm in his vision while being adaptable to changes in detail. This approach has made Amazon an agile company that makes prompt decisions to maintain its leadership position. Amazon's managers have access to various internal systems that allow them to make swift choices which shape the company's future. Andy Jassy, now CEO of Amazon, played a crucial role in developing the organisation's cloud platform under Bezos' guidance. Furthermore, Bezos is skilled at choosing competent leaders such as Jassy who holds himself and others accountable for Amazon's high standards, ensuring they do not become mediocre and retain what makes them exceptional. This attribute sealed his appointment as CEO according to Bezos when he said: **'I guarantee that Andy will never let the universe make us typical.'**

Bezos effectively formed a Management Team who shared the same passion and dedication towards realising Amazon's vision and has worked alongside them throughout the years to propel the company to its current level of achievement. This teamwork among like-minded leaders with shared goals is a fundamental tactic that contributes greatly to the immense success of the business.

Amazon continually experiments with concepts before narrowing down their choices to what works best. The company does not shy away from taking risks in pursuing product or service development, even if there exists an inherent chance of failure associated with such ventures.

In short, Amazon has shown that constant reinvention can help a company not just stay relevant in the industry but that it also has the huge potential to make it a leader in the industry. By having a leadership team that shares the same vision and strategy, innovating using technology but keeping the focus on its customer's needs and continually experimenting, Amazon has been able to stay ahead of the curve has remained one of the most successful companies in the world today. It is interesting to see what they will launch next!

'To be innovative, you have to experiment. If you want to have more invention, you need to do more experiments per week per month per year per decade, it's that simple. You cannot invent without experimenting and here's the other thing about experiments, lots of them fail. If you know it's gonna work in advance it is not an experiment.'

- Jeff Bezos, CEO, Amazon

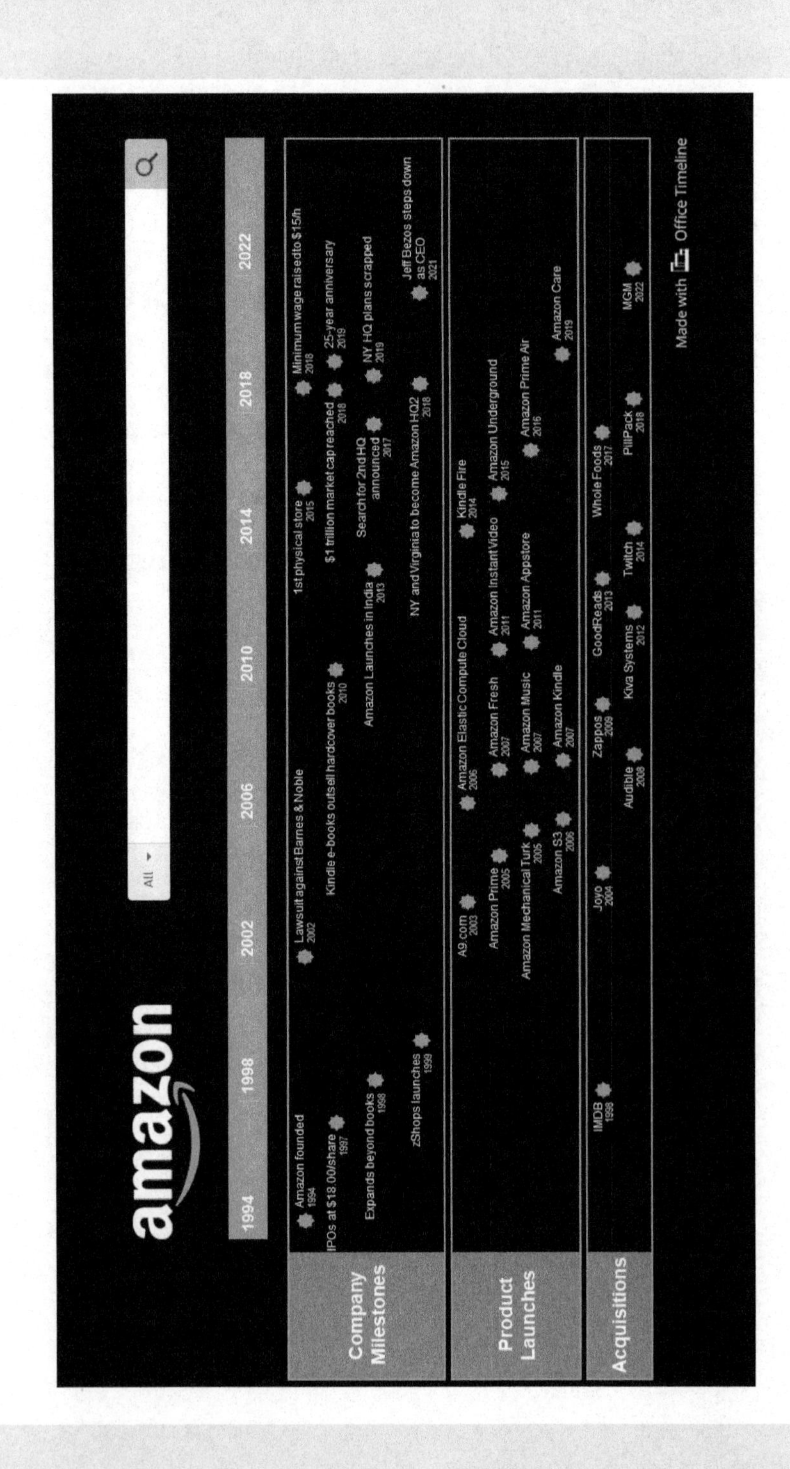
amazon
All
1994
1998
2002
2006
2010
2014
2018
2022
Company Milestones
Amazon founded 1994
IPOs at $18.00/share 1997
Expands beyond books 1998
zShops launches 1999
Lawsuit against Barnes & Noble 2002
Kindle e-books outsell hardcover books 2010
Amazon Launches in India 2013
NY and Virginia to become Amazon HQ2 2018
1st physical store 2015
$1 trillion market cap reached 2018
Search for 2nd HQ announced 2017
Minimum wage raised to $15/h 2018
25-year anniversary 2019
NY HQ plans scrapped 2019
Jeff Bezos steps down as CEO 2021
Product Launches
A9.com 2003
Amazon Prime 2005
Amazon Mechanical Turk 2005
Amazon S3 2006
Amazon Elastic Compute Cloud 2006
Amazon Fresh 2007
Amazon Music 2007
Amazon Kindle 2007
Amazon Instant Video 2011
Amazon Appstore 2011
Kindle Fire 2014
Amazon Underground 2015
Amazon Prime Air 2016
Amazon Care 2019
Acquisitions
IMDB 1998
Joyo 2004
Zappos 2009
Audible 2008
GoodReads 2013
Kiva Systems 2012
Twitch 2014
Whole Foods 2017
PillPack 2018
MGM 2022
Made with Office Timeline

12

The Future

The success of any organisation hinges on its ability to constantly evolve and remain ahead of the curve. However, with an ever-increasing rate at which new technologies surface, it has become increasingly challenging for companies to stay abreast, let alone implement these technological advances in their operations.

Amongst the latest breakthroughs that could play a pivotal role in shaping a business's future include concepts such as artificial intelligence (AI), the metaverse and blockchain. Although countless other concepts exist or are being developed currently, our focus for this chapter will be on these three innovations. In this section, the significance of their contribution to shaping the future of business will be outlined. It is highly recommended that one pays attention since these emerging technologies are paving the way for future advancements and companies who fail to adapt may fall behind in their industries.

Artificial Intelligence (AI)

Artificial Intelligence (AI) has been creating an impact on numerous fields and its benefits are evident. What is AI? Artificial intelligence is the simulation of human intelligence processes by machines, especially computer systems. AI enables technical systems to perceive their environment, deal with what they perceive, solve problems and act to achieve a specific goal. A subset of artificial intelligence is Machine Learning (ML), which refers to computer programmes automatically learning from and adapting to new data without being assisted by humans. Deep learning techniques enable this automatic learning through the absorption of huge amounts of unstructured data such as text, images, or videos.

The concept of AI is founded on the idea that a machine can replicate human intelligence and perform tasks ranging from basic to extremely intricate ones. The main objective of this technology is to imitate cognitive activities like those carried out by humans. Remarkable progress has been made by experts in emulating functions like reasoning, learning, and perception which can be defined with clarity.

Generative AI is a type of AI that produces novel outputs using the data with which it has been trained. Unlike conventional AI systems, which recognise patterns and provide predictions, generative AI generates fresh content in various forms such as images, audio clips, or texts. Generative Adversarial Networks (GANs), a form of deep learning approach specifically designed for creating new content, are used by Generative AI. A GAN system comprises two neural networks: a generator responsible for generating fresh data and an evaluator which assesses its accuracy, working together to produce high-quality outputs similar to real-world information through constant feedback from each other until achieving indistinguishable results from actual ones.

AI is already being used in many areas of business, including customer service, marketing, and supply chain management. By analysing large amounts of data, AI can identify patterns and insights that humans may miss, which can lead to more informed decision-making and better outcomes. In customer service, AI-powered chatbots and virtual assistants can help businesses improve response times and provide personalised support to customers.

Generative AI takes this a step further by allowing machines to create novel and unique outputs based on specific inputs. This technology is particularly useful in product design and development, where businesses can create entirely new products or modify existing ones to meet specific customer needs. In marketing, generative AI can be used to create personalised content that resonates with target audiences.

Companies have realised the significance of data and its role in decision-making; hence AI has become crucial for any business. Its application is set to further expand within the business world. Here are some instances demonstrating how AI is currently employed.

Automating processes – AI is employed to automate monotonous duties that were formerly carried out by individuals. This not only conserves time but also minimises mistakes. An example would be customer service chatbots utilising AI to offer round-the-clock assistance to patrons without human involvement. Additionally, financial establishments use software powered by AI to mechanise their anti-fraud procedures.

Predictive analytics – AI is utilised to examine massive amounts of information with the objective of detecting patterns and foreseeing future occurrences. One illustration of this can be observed in e-commerce enterprises where AI is implemented to scrutinise consumer data, ultimately leading to personalised product suggestions. Furthermore, predictive maintenance propelled by AI presents another instance of how corporations are implementing it to anticipate equipment breakdowns beforehand which then diminishes upkeep costs and downtime expenditures.

Natural Language Processing (NLP) – NLP is a subfield of AI that deals with the interaction between humans and computers using natural language. It is used to analyse text data and extract insights from it. One of the most common applications of NLP is sentiment analysis which helps businesses gauge public opinion about their brand or products. NLP is also used in chatbots to understand customer queries and provide relevant responses.

Image and speech recognition – AI technology is currently being utilised to identify visual and vocal elements in order to carry out tasks that would typically require human assistance. An example of this can be seen in retail settings where AI cameras are used for inventory management by recognising when products need replenishment. Additionally, virtual assistants such as Siri and Alexa incorporate AI in their systems to comprehend and address user inquiries.

Autonomous systems – Autonomous systems are capable of functioning without human involvement. Self-driving cars, powered by AI sensors for steering and obstacle avoidance, serve as an illustration of autonomous systems. The application of autonomous technology in manufacturing and logistics automates processes while minimising the necessity for human intervention.

Decision-making – The utilisation of AI is aiding decision-making procedures by offering analysis-based insights and recommendations. Business intelligence software fuelled by AI can scrutinise data from diverse origins to furnish executives with an understanding of their company's progress, while investment platforms driven by AI can suggest investments based on analysed data.

Generative AI is now frequently utilised in the business world for product design and development. By leveraging generative AI, businesses can produce new and creative products or make alterations to current ones that cater to specific customer requirements. This technique is especially advantageous in industries like fashion, aerospace, and automotive where form and function are equally important factors.

Nike is an example of a corporation that has incorporated generative AI into their procedure for designing and developing products. They employ this technology to create shoe designs that are not only one-of-a-kind but also offer greater comfort and durability compared to their previous traditional footwear models. The utilisation of generative AI enables Nike to produce designs tailored to specific customer requirements and preferences, leading eventually to improved client gratification. Nike has successfully combined customer care with artificial intelligence, as evidenced by their Augmented Reality Design System patent acquisition in 2015. This allowed them to incorporate holographic technology into sneaker design. In April 2018, they also acquired computer vision firm, Invertex Ltd, further expanding their digital platform capabilities and complementing their purchase of analytics and consumer data company Zodiac Inc.

The Nike flagship store in New York has an extensive understanding of its customers who use their app and enter the store, including their preferred colours, favoured sports, shoe size and other details. Nike's strategy for customer involvement employs this data to create a customised shopping experience that is top-notch. This information gathered through the app assists Nike with determining which shoes should be sold in any particular retail outlet as well as guiding future decision-making for the company at large.

Generative AI is finding its way into the business world through the development of marketing materials like advertisements, logos and social media posts. Companies can now use generative AI to craft distinctive and customised content that connects with their intended audience, a critical aspect in today's digital age where businesses need to differentiate themselves from competitors. Generative Ai is also making the whole process much faster.

The release of 'Create Real Magic' by Coca-Cola is indicative of the growing importance of generative AI in marketing. This project was developed through a recent collaboration between consultant Bain & Company and OpenAI, with Coke being the first to utilise this partnership for their marketing efforts. The company has shown optimism about the potential benefits that generative AI can offer in advertising.

'Coca-Cola is still in the early days of assessing AI's potential impact. We're just scratching the surface of what we believe will help create the industry's most effective and efficient end-to-end marketing model.'

- Manolo Arroyo, Global Chief Marketing Officer at Coke

The financial sector has also started utilising AI, particularly in fraud detection and prevention. By examining large amounts of transaction data with this technology, financial institutions can detect suspicious patterns that may indicate fraudulent activities. With online banking and e-commerce leading to a rise in such activities, AI proves useful for preventing them. JPMorgan Chase is among the companies incorporating AI into their fraud detection measures. The bank leverages this technology to scrutinise transaction data to identify potential fraudulent actions swiftly and accurately.

With the increasing adoption of AI and generative AI in businesses, it is likely that we will witness more revolutionary developments and advancements which will revolutionise our lifestyle and work. These technologies are progressively significant to enable businesses to remain competitive and adjust according to shifting market circumstances. Businesses that do not integrate these cutting-edge technologies into their operations run the risk of lagging behind their more resourceful competitors thereby losing their market dominance.

Generative AI's evolution

For an advanced technology that's considered relatively new, generative AI is deep-rooted in history and innovation.

1932
Georges Artsrouni invents a machine he reportedly called the "**mechanical brain**" to translate between languages on a mechanical computer encoded onto punch cards.

1957
Linguist **Noam Chomsky** publishes ***Syntactic Structures***, which describes grammatical rules for parsing and generating natural language sentences.

1966
MIT professor Joseph Weizenbaum creates the first chatbot, **Eliza**, which simulates conversations with a psychotherapist.

1968
Computer science professor Terry Winograd creates SHRDLU, the first multimodal AI that can manipulate and reason out a world of blocks according to instructions from a user.

1980
Michael Toy and Glenn Wichman develop the Unix-based game *Rogue*, which uses procedural content generation to dynamically generate new game levels.

1985
Computer scientist and philosopher Judea Pearl introduces Bayesian networks causal analysis, which provides statistical techniques for representing uncertainty that leads to methods for generating content in a specific style, tone or length.

1986
Michael Irwin Jordan lays the foundation for the modern use of recurrent neural networks (RNNs) with the publication of "Serial order: a parallel distributed processing approach."

1989
Yann LeCun, Yoshua Bengio and Patrick Haffner demonstrate how convolutional neural networks (CNNs) can be used to recognize images.

2000
University of Montreal researchers publish "A Neural Probabilistic Language Model," which suggests a method to model language using feed-forward neural networks.

2006
Data scientist Fei-Fei Li sets up the ImageNet database, which provides the foundation for visual object recognition.

2011
Apple releases **Siri**, a voice-powered personal assistant that can generate responses and take actions in response to voice requests.

2012
Alex Krizhevsky designs the AlexNet CNN architecture, pioneering a new way of automatically training neural networks that take advantage of recent GPU advances.

2013
Google researcher Tomas Mikolov and colleagues introduce word2vec to identify semantic relationships between words automatically.

2014
Research scientist **Ian Goodfellow** develops generative adversarial networks (GANs), which pit two neural networks against each other to generate increasingly realistic content.

Diederik Kingma and Max Welling introduce variational autoencoders to generate images, videos and text.

2015
Stanford researchers publish work on diffusion models in the paper **"Deep Unsupervised Learning using Nonequilibrium Thermodynamics."** The technique provides a way to reverse-engineer the process of adding noise to a final image.

2017
Google researchers develop the concept of transformers in the seminal paper "Attention is all you need," inspiring subsequent research into tools that could automatically parse unlabeled text into large language models (LLMs).

2018
Google researchers implement transformers into BERT, which is trained on more than 3.3 billion words and can automatically learn the relationship between words in sentences, paragraphs and even books to predict the meaning of text. It has 110 million parameters.

Google DeepMind researchers develop AlphaFold for predicting protein structures, laying the foundation for generative AI applications in medical research, drug development and chemistry.

OpenAI releases GPT (Generative Pre-trained Transformer). Trained on about 40 gigabytes of data and consisting of 117 million parameters, GPT paves the way for subsequent LLMs in content generation, chatbots and language translation.

2021
OpenAI introduces **Dall-E**, which can generate images from text prompts. The name is a combination of WALL-E, the name of a fictional robot, and the artist Salvador Dali.

2022
Researchers from Runway Research, Stability AI and CompVis LMU release Stable Diffusion as open source code that can automatically generate image content from a text prompt.

OpenAI releases **ChatGPT** in November to provide a chat-based interface to its GPT 3.5 LLM. It attracts over 100 million users within two months, representing the fastest ever consumer adoption of a service.

2023
Getty Images and a group of artists separately sue several companies that implemented Stable Diffusion for copyright infringement.

Microsoft integrates a version of ChatGPT into its Bing search engine. Google quickly follows with plans to release the Bard chat service based on its Lamda engine. And the controversy over detecting AI-generated content heats up.

Metaverse

If you are wondering what the metaverse is, you are not alone. No one can give you a complete answer because it has not been totally invented, it is still in development. Its fully built form is not yet known. What we know is that it is a virtual, immersive world. It is three-dimensional and much more absorbing, decentralised, based on blockchain and operates on token-based economics.

Decentralised – In simple terms, decentralisation is a system or network that functions without any central control. It operates as a peer-to-peer network where all devices and computers connected to it have an equal role in its operation. The absence of one centralised authority makes the system more robust and resilient against potential failures or attacks. Moreover, because data is stored on multiple nodes instead of one single location, decentralisation provides increased privacy and security for users.

Token Based Economics – Token-based economics refers to the creation of an economic system that employs digital tokens as a medium for exchanging, storing value and motivating individuals. These tokens can represent anything with significant worth, including commodities, currency, or access rights to products/services. In such an economic model, these tokens are utilised in trading goods and services; their market demand determines their corresponding values. Furthermore, they also serve as incentives for certain behaviours and actions like participating in networks or contributing to specific projects.

The Metaverse holds the promise of transforming various sectors such as entertainment, education, and commerce. Its potential in revolutionising the way people consume digital content like gaming is enormous by providing a highly immersive experience. In addition to that, it can also offer an interactive platform for students to learn through hands-on approaches.

Similarly, businesses stand to benefit from the ability of the Metaverse to create new ways of engaging with their customers while selling their products or services online. According to recent research, about half of U.S. consumers aged 18-34 have accessed the Metaverse, but nearly half of the younger demographic is still unfamiliar with the concept. In the U.S. alone, the average monthly number of searches on the Metaverse is 480,000.

Now is the time that the biggest players in the Metaverse and Web 3.0 space are:

- testing virtual experiences,
- improving baseline technology
- building talent for this future.

It is expected that in five to seven years, the Metaverse will not be tied to a specific world, like Decentraland or Roblox. Instead, the Metaverse will be an extension of any experience layer. Any website or digital experience will have an augmented reality/virtual reality (AR/VR) component and will exist on the new Web 3.0 iteration of internet technology. Gartner predicts that by 2026, 25% of people will spend at least an hour a day in the Metaverse. Immersive VR technology will change the way we do business, study, socialise and pay bills. A new era is coming for sure, but in my opinion not as fast as it might seem.

The Metaverse is still in an early stage of development and technology is not ready yet. It is difficult to predict which channels and areas will be worth investing in. But if a company does not want to miss out on the opportunities this technology has to offer, it is crucial to start preparing and finding its place in this space. Think about:

Talent base - what skillset will your team need to be able to experiment and learn from using the metaverse.

Future-proof your tech stack – composable commerce – based on the principles of MACH (microservices, API-first, cloud-native and headless) to become more agile and future-proof.

Simplifying the customer journey – user-friendly design, personalisation, localisation, frictionless purchasing experience.

Embrace the growing amount of data – use of AI.

Test, Test and Test – keep experimenting!

With so many options, organisations should expand their focus from simply focusing on whether to sell in the Metaverse to how to do so in a differentiated manner. Some areas that businesses should look into are immersive marketing and events, NFT based loyalty programs, product testing and virtual try-ons, blockchain verification, optimised digital and physical integration.

Augmented store experiences are one of the most important use cases. The Metaverse offers an opportunity for businesses to develop virtual renditions of their merchandise, providing customers with a more engaging and immersive experience in contrast to conventional online shopping. To illustrate, car manufacturers could establish a virtual showroom where clients can interact with digital versions of cars, personalise them according to their preferences, and even undertake simulated test drives. Utilising the Metaverse for product demonstrations may create more lasting impressions on consumers while increasing sales figures and fostering brand loyalty.

A company should not invest in the Metaverse just because it is in the news or because other companies are doing it. You should invest because you understand who your consumers are, and because you know your consumer is on that platform or going to be on that platform. A growing number of companies are buying up space in the Metaverse so that they can set up shop there. These firms include the likes of Adidas, Burberry, Gucci, Tommy Hilfiger, Nike, Samsung and Louis Vuitton. Retail and luxury goods brands have already launched their projects in the Metaverse environment. For example, in Nikeland, a micro-metaverse space built on the Roblox platform, Nike allowed users to try virtual products when playing games.

Gucci is proving that there is real money to be made in virtual goods. The Italian fashion house has offered a wide range of digital items for sale in 2021, from $13 virtual sneakers to a unique Roblox handbag that resold for more than $4,000 and a video NFT auctioned by Christie's for $25,000. This proves that these collaborations that the virtual world can create a very significant new revenue stream. Another example of retail-games cooperation is Balenciaga which created a virtual store in the Fortnite game. The virtual store replicated the brand's physical stores.

However, there are still a lot of challenges for businesses to adopt the technology. More than half of consumers are worried about harassment, inclusion, and data privacy in the Metaverse and expect brands to address these Web 2.0 issues before the adoption of Web 3.0. Research shows that most consumers are not on Metaverse platforms—yet. Retailers should first get their current 2.0 social media strategies right first, to ensure they translate to Web 3.0 and appeal to young consumers' need for authenticity. As we move further into the digital world, it is important for brands to focus on creating emotionally appealing retail experiences. In the Metaverse, this means using sight and sound to create a space that feels as real as possible. Companies should also start thinking about their talent base, to upskill employees and build Web 3.0 talent.

Interoperability will be crucial. The Metaverse is comprises multiple worlds, and it is unclear if individuals will be able to easily 'travel' and bring expensive digital goods among them. Broadband enablement is another challenge. Most consumers lack full access to the more advanced technology and services needed to run a Metaverse environment. Trust is also an important topic in the virtual world. Attempts to illegally profit from NFTs and lawsuits between companies trying to stake claims in the Metaverse may hinder public trust in this new technology.

User experience will play an important role. Aspects of the Metaverse today feel clunky and cartoonish, potentially causing many consumers to lose interest after the initial novelty wears off.

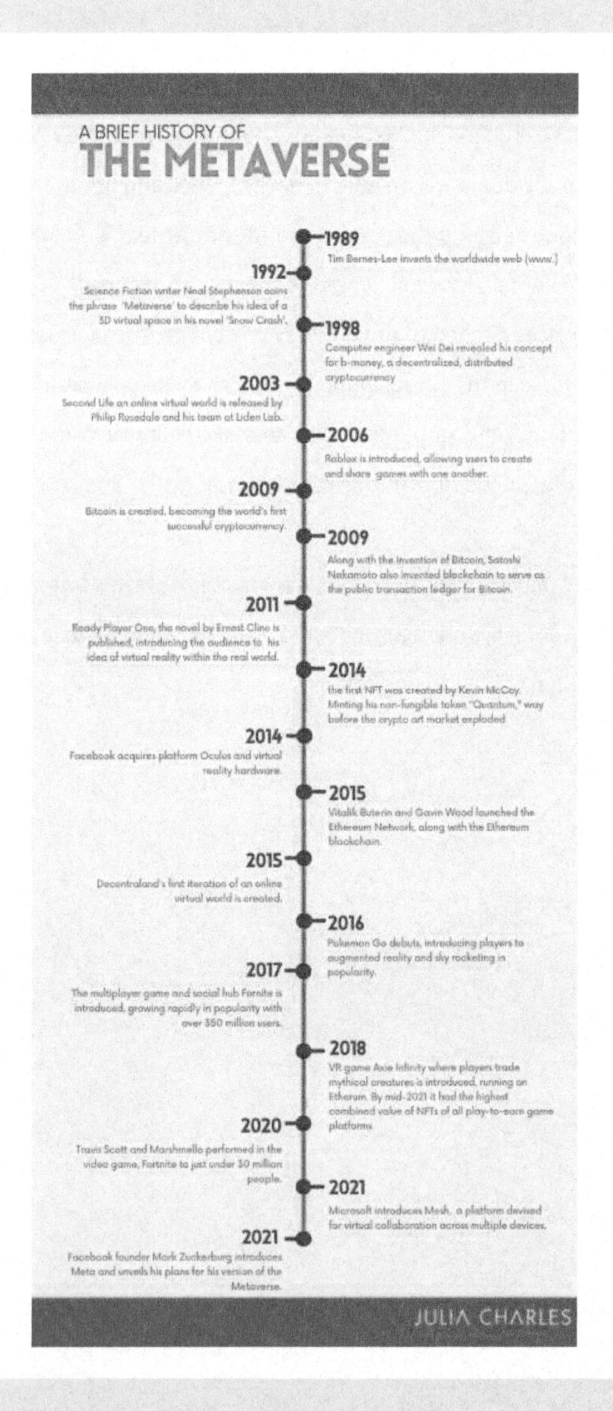
A BRIEF HISTORY OF
THE METAVERSE
1989
Tim Bernes-Lee invents the worldwide web (www.)
1992
Science Fiction writer Neal Stephenson coins the phrase 'Metaverse' to describe his idea of a 3D virtual space in his novel 'Snow Crash'.
1998
Computer engineer Wei Dei revealed his concept for b-money, a decentralized, distributed cryptocurrency
2003
Second Life an online virtual world is released by Philip Rosedale and his team at Liden Lab.
2006
Roblox is introduced, allowing users to create and share games with one another.
2009
Bitcoin is created, becoming the world's first successful cryptocurrency.
2009
Along with the Invention of Bitcoin, Satoshi Nakamoto also invented blockchain to serve as the public transaction ledger for Bitcoin.
2011
Ready Player One, the novel by Ernest Cline is published, introducing the audience to his idea of virtual reality within the real world.
2014
the first NFT was created by Kevin McCoy. Minting his non-fungible token "Quantum," way before the crypto art market exploded
2014
Facebook acquires platform Oculus and virtual reality hardware.
2015
Vitalik Buterin and Gavin Wood launched the Ethereum Network, along with the Ethereum blockchain.
2015
Decentraland's first iteration of an online virtual world is created.
2016
Pokemon Go debuts, introducing players to augmented reality and sky rocketing in popularity.
2017
The multiplayer game and social hub Fornite is introduced, growing rapidly in popularity with over 350 million users.
2018
VR game Axie Infinity where players trade mythical creatures is introduced, running on Etherum. By mid-2021 it had the highest combined value of NFTs of all play-to-earn game platforms
2020
Travis Scott and Marshmello performed in the video game, Fortnite to just under 30 million people.
2021
Microsoft introduces Mesh, a platform devised for virtual collaboration across multiple devices.
2021
Facebook founder Mark Zuckerburg introduces Meta and unveils his plans for his version of the Metaverse.
JULIA CHARLES

Blockchain

In recent years, there has been widespread discussion about blockchain, bitcoins and cryptocurrencies. Despite this, many people are still uncertain about the concept and its functionality. In essence, blockchain is a technique used for data storage where information is kept in blocks that are connected to previous ones. These blocks consist of a list of transactions, a distinctive identifier called hash for all the data within the block as well as hash of preceding block's data.

The content within a block generally includes transactions which could range from several dollars to hundreds of dollars. For instance, if Jack transfers $100 to Jill, it would be regarded as one of the numerous transactions in a block. A hash is an exclusive mix of digits and characters that serve as an identifier for the information present in each blockchain's blocks; just like fingerprints do for individuals. Every block on the chain has its unique hash value which changes when data contained therein undergoes modifications. Therefore, changing the transaction amount from $100 to $50 between Jack and Jill would cause complete alteration of the associated block's hash value. To form a chain structure among multiple blocks on this platform, every subsequent piece must contain references or hashes linked with prior ones accordingly. Thus, creating what we call 'blockchain.'

If there is any modification made in a transaction within a block, it will result in a change of the block's hash. This alteration then leads to mismatched hashes with the previously recorded ones by subsequent blocks. As such, blockchain technology gains its tamper-resistant feature due to its ability to detect data changes effortlessly. Furthermore, another aspect that enhances blockchain security is how it stores information across numerous computers on a peer-to-peer network rather than relying on one central server or computer like traditional banking databases. Each node within this network possesses an identical copy of the entire blockchain system.

"Miners" are self-sufficient and interconnected entities that utilise their computing power to verify transactions before appending them to the blockchain. Whenever a new block of transactions is required to be added, all nodes within the network must examine and authenticate each transaction in the block for validity. When all nodes unanimously agree on accuracy, this newly formed block will become part of every node's blockchain through consensus. Consequently, anyone attempting to manipulate data stored in a blockchain would need access to most computers across its peer-to-peer network since it represents an unbreakable security measure against tampering with any information contained therein.

To conduct a transaction on a blockchain, users are provided with both public and private keys by the software. These keys, like hashes, consist of random combinations of letters and numbers generated by the software itself. It is crucial for users to safeguard their private key and avoid sharing it with anyone else while they can freely share their public key like an email ID which allows others to send messages. The analogy of a mailbox illustrates this point where the private key serves as a password allowing only you access whereas your public key functions like an address that enables others to send messages your way. Moreover, each type of key has its own unique characteristics such as using the private key for digital signature creation purposes.

A digital signature is essentially a combination of characters and numbers, but the unique aspect lies in its verification process. The corresponding public key enables anyone to authenticate whether the message was genuinely signed by the sender using their public key or not. In blockchain, this cryptography involving both keys and message signing results in what we know as digital signatures.

There are three broad categories of blockchain depending upon who can access them.

Public blockchains refer to databases that are open for anyone to access, copy and modify based on consensus. A classic example of a public blockchain is Bitcoin. These types of blockchains operate in a fully decentralised manner, allowing new participants to join the network at any time with equal rights as existing members. All parties can validate blocks and access data contained within them without restriction or permission requirements. The main benefit of public blockchains lies in their pure decentralisation while the downside may be slower transaction processing compared to other blockchain models.

Managed or private blockchains are tightly controlled systems that are centrally managed and regulated, providing restricted access. They require a central authority to determine who can become a node and grant the rights to modify or access the database. Not all nodes have equal privileges, with blocks being verified by either empowered nodes or centralised authorities. The right to read data is also determined by this central body. Hence these blockchains are known as permissioned ones. Essentially functioning like regular databases in terms of limited accessibility, they employ blockchain technology for implementation purposes only.

As such, there is no need for activities like mining blocks or validation since the system can be accessed only by select individuals or organisations intending to share data privately amongst themselves. Credit Mutuel Arkea has implemented this strategy of using private blockchain successfully in sharing information within its subsidiaries while Ripple serves as another example of such an approach employed through their blockchain platform. This blockchain boasts a swifter performance compared to others as it eliminates the burdens of mining and consensus. However, its major drawback lies in deviating from decentralisation principles, appearing more akin to conventional systems due to tight control measures.

Hybrid or consortium blockchains are a type of permissioned blockchain where control is shared among a group of organisations rather than just one, like private blockchains. They fall somewhere between public and private blockchains with more restrictions compared to the former but less restrictive than the latter. This flexibility has earned them their other name: hybrid blockchains. Consortium members come to consensus on accepting new nodes while blocks must adhere to predefined rules established by the consortium for validation purposes. Access rights can be either public or restricted depending on certain node privileges and user rights may vary per individual which makes these types of blockchains partially decentralised in nature.

The hybrid blockchain merges the pros and cons of public and private blockchains, occupying the middle ground between complete centralisation and full decentralisation. While it offers quicker response times than public counterparts, its speed falls short of that offered by private blockchains. However, this type of blockchain operates subject to cooperation within the consortium. Any rejection could negatively impact its functionality.

The emergence of blockchain technology offers a hopeful remedy to several challenges confronted by modern businesses. From financial transactions to supply chain management, blockchain can transform conventional business practices. Supply chain management presents one of the most promising applications for this technology as it enables companies to establish a transparent and secure system that eliminates risks such as fraud and counterfeiting in their operations. By tracking product origin, quality, and movement through blockchain ledgers, customers can be assured of receiving authentic high-quality products from businesses utilising this innovation.

Blockchain technology has the potential to be utilised in financial transactions by creating a safe and visible method of transferring funds and carrying out transactions. By removing intermediaries, blockchain's decentralised structure minimises the risk of fraud while decreasing transaction costs connected with conventional financial systems. Blockchain technology also has potential applications in identity management, offering a decentralised and secure method for storing personal information. By utilising blockchain in this field, organisations can establish a more secure system that is less susceptible to data breaches or hacking attempts. Furthermore, voting systems could also leverage blockchain as an audit trail to ensure the authenticity of elections by creating transparency and immunity against tampering activities.

Blockchain technology also has the potential to revolutionise a business by facilitating the creation of new business models. Decentralised Autonomous Organisations (DAOs) are one such innovation that employs computer programmes instead of human managers to govern operations. These DAOs can offer more effective and economical solutions compared to traditional models. An instance is a decentralised ride-sharing platform where intermediaries are not necessary, thereby reducing costs for drivers and passengers alike.

Blockchain technology can be used in applications for smart contract development. Such contracts are designed to self-execute when specific conditions are met, allowing for automation of the contracting process, reducing intermediary involvement. This can lead to increased efficiency and may be applicable across various fields, including finance and supply chain management.

To sum up, blockchain technology can revolutionise the way companies function by offering a safe, clear, and decentralised platform for managing records, financial transactions and identities. Through utilising blockchain technology, businesses have opportunities to establish fresh business models while enhancing effectiveness and minimising expenses. As this technology progresses, we anticipate an increase in its usage among more organisations as they tap its potential for fostering innovation and expansion.

The emergence of AI, the Metaverse, and Blockchain have paved the way for new advancements in digital transformation. These technologies possess remarkable capabilities to enhance industries, optimise productivity, and introduce fresh approaches to conducting businesses. Neglecting these innovative technologies may result in companies falling behind as society progresses towards newer methodologies. As a business owner or manager, it is crucial to begin exploring these emerging technologies and identifying ways in which they can propel your enterprise forward. Early adopters of such tools will gain a significant edge over their rivals and reap the numerous advantages that come with them. Conversely, ignoring these innovations may result in being outpaced by competitors who embrace them and use them as an advantage.

It is crucial to highlight that embracing novel technologies is not solely aimed at gaining a competitive edge. It also pertains to remaining relevant and fulfilling the demands of consumers. With relentless advancement in technology, consumer expectations are being transformed, and enterprises capable of adapting are more probable to thrive in the long haul.

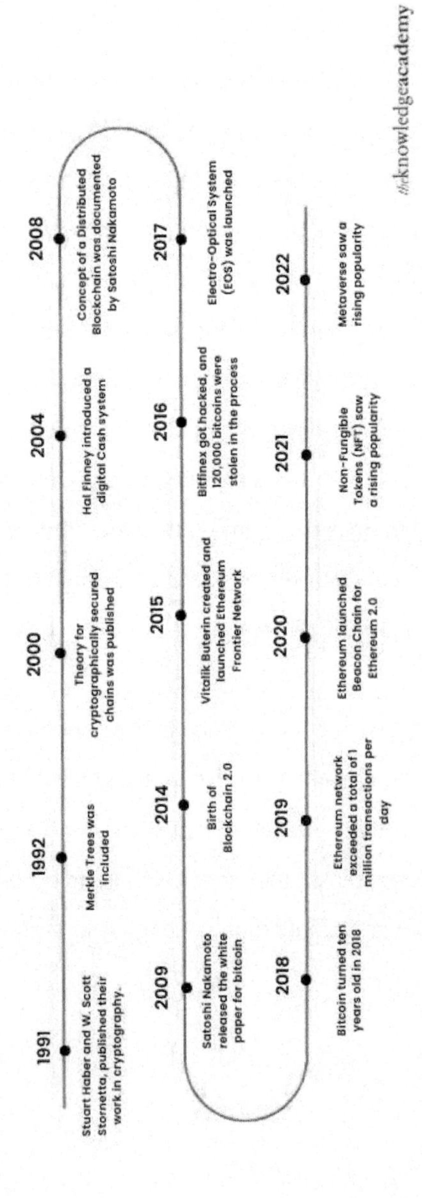
Blockchain History Timeline
1991
Stuart Haber and W. Scott Stornetta, published their work in cryptography.
1992
Merkle Trees was included
2000
Theory for cryptographically secured chains was published
2004
Hal Finney introduced a digital Cash system
2008
Concept of a Distributed Blockchain was documented by Satoshi Nakamoto
2009
Satoshi Nakamoto released the white paper for bitcoin
2014
Birth of Blockchain 2.0
2015
Vitalik Buterin created and launched Ethereum Frontier Network
2016
Bitfinex got hacked, and 120,000 bitcoins were stolen in the process
2017
Electro-Optical System (EOS) was launched
2018
Bitcoin turned ten years old in 2018
2019
Ethereum network exceeded a total of 1 million transactions per day
2020
Ethereum launched Beacon Chain for Ethereum 2.0
2021
Non-Fungible Tokens (NFT) saw a rising popularity
2022
Metaverse saw a rising popularity
theknowledgeacademy

OPEN AI: CHATGPT

ChatGPT, a language model created by OpenAI and powered by AI technology generates human-like responses in conversational format. This 'chat' model also performs various language tasks such as translation, summarisation, question answering and more.

ChatGPT4 is the most recent advancement in the GPT series of language models that uses Generative Pre-Trained Transformer technology developed by OpenAI. With its unparalleled amount of training data, it stands out as an exceptional Natural Language Processing (NLP) model which can generate realistic responses for diverse prompts and enquiries. The GPT series of models has already had a significant impact on the field of NLP, with applications ranging from chatbots and virtual assistants to language translation and content creation. However, ChatGPT4 takes this technology to the next level, with improved accuracy, larger training datasets and more sophisticated language models.

Why is ChatGPT4 important for businesses? The answer lies in the growing importance of NLP and AI-powered chatbots in customer service and engagement. As more and more businesses shift to online channels and e-commerce, there is a growing need for chatbots and virtual assistants that can provide fast, efficient, and personalised customer service.

By utilising ChatGPT4, businesses can transform their customer interactions by offering a conversational experience that is more authentic and human-like. This advanced technology empowers enterprises to design chatbots and digital assistants capable of instantly comprehending and addressing customers' inquiries without any human involvement.

Here are a few examples on how businesses can leverage this technology.

Customer Service Chatbots – One of the most apparent uses of ChatGPT4 for enterprises is in creating chatbots for customer service. With ChatGPT4, companies can produce chatbots that comprehend and address client enquiries more naturally and humanely. This may enhance customer contentment by providing quicker and more effective answers to their questions.

Virtual Assistants – The utilisation of ChatGPT4 extends to creating virtual assistants that aid consumers with various duties, such as booking appointments and presenting product suggestions. Employing the capabilities of ChatGPT4 enables enterprises to establish virtual assistants capable of comprehending conversational language enquiries and furnishing customised answers founded on customer inclinations.

Content Creation – The ChatGPT4 model can produce excellent content for businesses. Utilising this model, businesses can fabricate a diverse array of material that encompasses blog posts, social media messages and descriptions about products or services as well as promotional scripts. This feature may enable companies to economise time and resources on crafting content while still ensuring top-notch and captivating content.

Personalised Marketing – With ChatGPT4, businesses can craft individualised marketing messages for their clients. By scrutinising customer information and employing the model to produce bespoke communications, companies can launch focused promotional initiatives that have a higher chance of connecting with their target audience.

Language Translation – The ChatGPT4 model can perform translation tasks, enabling businesses to interact with customers who speak different languages. Through text translation, companies can develop customer service chatbots and virtual assistants that offer assistance in multiple languages across the globe.

The innovative technology of ChatGPT4 revolutionises the way businesses interact with their customers. With this technology, companies can establish chatbots and virtual assistants that are capable of comprehending and answering customer enquiries more authentically, conserving time and resources on content creation and marketing. As online channels and e-commerce persist as a growing trend among businesses, NLP along with AI-powered chatbots will become even more crucial for staying competitive, making ChatGPT4 an essential tool for forward-thinking enterprises.

'AI's benefits for humankind could be so unbelievably good that it's hard for me to even imagine.'

- OpenAI CEO Sam Altman was quoted in The New York Times

OpenAI timeline

2015
OpenAI was officially founded

2016
OpenAI Gym was released

2018
OpenAI first introduces the concept of Generative Pre-Trained Transformer

2019
OpenAI shifts from nonprofit status to "capped profit" status

2021
OpenAI releases the first Dall-E generative AI model

2022
OpenAI releases Dall-E 2 and then ChatGPT later in the year

2023
Microsoft commits to multibillion-dollar investment in OpenAI and GPT-4 is released

13

Conclusion

The 11 chapters that I have covered in this book present some of the key concepts that businesses should consider understanding and adopting as part of their transformation journey. There is no doubt that there are many other factors that contribute to a successful business in this rapidly advancing world we live in; everyone holds diverse opinions on what holds more significance. The concepts covered in this book, if embraced and executed well by any business, would greatly benefit it.

Experimentation is a crucial aspect of transformation, as it allows organisations to innovate – quickly test and validate new ideas and approaches. This helps to minimise risk and increase the chances of success.

People are highly important in any transformation journey. You need the right people with the right attitude and skills on board if you want your organisation to make it through this process in one piece. That means having leaders who actually care about making change happen and a culture that is all about constantly growing and getting better.

If you want to be a game-changer in today's digital world, embracing innovation is the key. With its ability to birth fresh ideas and customer-oriented products, services and experiences that offer real value, organisations cannot afford to avoid innovating anymore. Partnering with external players like start-ups or investing in internal R&D efforts are crucial tactics for any organisation looking forward to staying ahead of the competition. Do not wait until your competitors make the first move - Innovate!

In recent times, the platform business model has gained significant traction as it offers a fresh perspective on how companies can generate and capitalise on value. Through establishing and managing platforms that facilitate collaboration among different entities such as businesses or individuals, organisations stand to leverage novel avenues for expansion and creativity.

In today's fast-moving and constantly changing world, it is essential to adopt a lean and agile business culture. This allows an organisation to quickly adjust and adopt to evolving market conditions, as well as regularly examining and enhancing its strategy.

Co-creation, building and or participating in an ecosystem are also critical components of digital transformation. By working with partners and other stakeholders, organisations can create new value propositions and customer experiences that would not have been possible to create alone.

Defining and putting a strategy into action is a crucial step that binds all components. To attain their intended results, organisations must possess an unambiguous and well-expressed strategy along with a method of implementing it effectively.

It is important to bear in mind that digital transformation entails a continuous process, where constantly innovating and introducing new business models are critical components. Whether due to the emergence of fresh technologies, market trends or shifts in customer behaviour, organisations need to be flexible and receptive to stay relevant and competitive in the digital era.

Thanks for taking the time to read this book. I hope it has provided you with a useful overview of this complex and rapidly evolving field, and that you make use of the insights and concepts presented here to help drive your own transformation journey.

If you have any questions or would like to learn more or would like just to share some thoughts (I am constantly learning new concepts whenever I talk to someone), feel free to reach out! I can be reached at jheeva@protinusgrp.com.

ALL THE BEST IN YOUR TRANSFORMATION JOURNEY!

14

Example of a Transformation Strategy - Retail

The illustration on page 285 is an example of a transformation strategy that was used for a large format retail business that was very traditional and losing relevance in the industry. The business had some fundamental issues:

No differentiation – sold the same products as their competitors and almost everything was sold at a discount to desperately maintain top line numbers which created a very bad identity for the business; being known as a dated and discounted store. This meant good international brands were wary of being associated with the retail outlet. There was no emphasis on private labels or exclusive brands.

No digital presence – No e-commerce channel, not present on social media channels (apart from promotional messages on Facebook), no focus on online advertising. This was in 2019!

Inadequate systems – The current back end system was vastly inadequate to run a retail business in the current times. The system was 19 years old and there was no real use of data intelligence to review the business let alone grow the business. No utilisation of data for analytics.

People - The business suffered from not having the right talent, especially when it came to areas such as e-commerce, digital marketing, product creation (private label), data analytics, visual merchandising, and human resource. Human resources was being run by the legal department, which meant no focus was being put on people strategy.

The transformation strategy was divided into four phases.

- Fundamental strategies
- Digital elements
- New business model
- Increase scale and scope

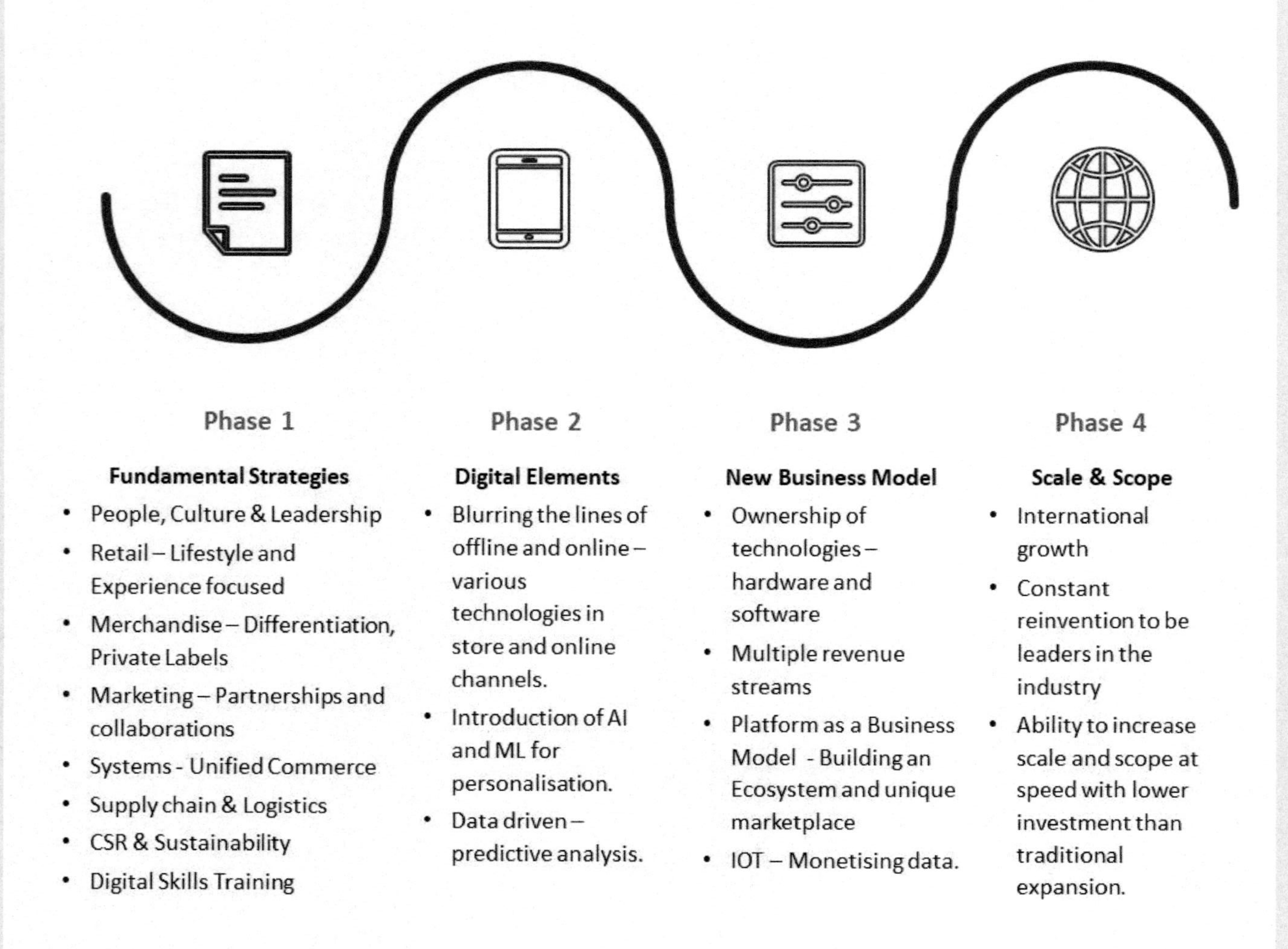
Phase 1
Fundamental Strategies
People, Culture & Leadership
Retail – Lifestyle and Experience focused
Merchandise – Differentiation, Private Labels
Marketing – Partnerships and collaborations
Systems - Unified Commerce
Supply chain & Logistics
CSR & Sustainability
Digital Skills Training
Phase 2
Digital Elements
Blurring the lines of offline and online – various technologies in store and online channels.
Introduction of AI and ML for personalisation.
Data driven – predictive analysis.
Phase 3
New Business Model
Ownership of technologies – hardware and software
Multiple revenue streams
Platform as a Business Model - Building an Ecosystem and unique marketplace
IOT – Monetising data.
Phase 4
Scale & Scope
International growth
Constant reinvention to be leaders in the industry
Ability to increase scale and scope at speed with lower investment than traditional expansion.

Phase 1 was to define the fundamental strategies by understanding where the business was, where it wanted to go and how it was going to be achieved. The plan was to work on a set of objectives and understand the challenges to achieve the objectives, define some guiding principles to overcome the challenges and then decide on action plans to execute the guiding policies.

Phase 2 saw the introduction of technology and digital concepts to help improve processes, execute the action plan and achieve the objectives.

Phase 3 was to ensure that the business leveraged technology and improved processes to evolve into a new business model with new revenue streams together with embracing the co-creation and ecosystem concepts.

Phase 4 was to then to ensure that there was a process of constant reinvention and to increase scale and scope of the new business model.

Unfortunately, despite best efforts, the transformation project did not achieve its goals. A study by Capgemini found that 70% of digital transformation projects fail to meet their objectives, while other studies have reported failure rates as high as 85%. This particular transformation project saw small wins throughout its implementation phase but as it was not completed, in my view, it was not a successful transformation. There were many reasons for this but some of the key factors were:

Lack of stakeholder buy-in – Digital transformation projects require alignment of objectives throughout the organisation, from shareholders to every employee in the organisation. In this case, there was no alignment on the transformation objectives between management and shareholders.

Lack of resource – The company, struggled to initiate change as the shareholders were not committed to the transformation project. Therefore not supporting the project with the investment needed. Due to budget constraints, the company had to find alternative ways to support the changes, which meant sometimes not being able to get the best solutions. It also could not hire individuals with sufficient skill sets to ensure that it was getting the best out of the technologies being introduced.

People strategy – despite a constant reminder that there was a desperate need to reform the culture of the organisation, this unfortunately was never given priority.

Not customer centric – for any transformation project to succeed, it must be centred around creating value for the customer. Unfortunately, the lack of resources and skill set meant that most of the ideas were internally generated (in-out organisation) rather than acting on data derived from customer journeys, preferences, etc.

Personally, it was a learning experience for myself on how to approach a transformation project and also what to prioritise and how to structure the transformation project. This is the basis on which I have approached this book.

DIGITAL TRANSFORMATION STEPS

IT'S A JOURNEY

Constant Re-Invention

- Digital Transformation is an ever evolving journey.
- Constant eye toward the future is the nature of digital business transformation

New Business Model

- Evolve to a new business model leveraging technology

Digital Transformation Strategy & Implementation

- Clear Strategy and Objectives
- Lean & Agile Approach
- Co-Creation and Ecosystem

Digital Leadership

- Functional Organisations – Value Networks
- Mindset - All In
- Top to Down Buy In
- Change management – Prioritise People Strategy
- Culture of Experimentation and Innovation

Case Study

I will end this book with a story about YouTube, like a play's final act, when all the characters, themes, and stories come together.

YouTube: From a Startup to a Global Sensation

Few could have predicted that online video would become a dominant entertainment and communication medium in the early days. The digital media landscape was forever altered with the launch in 2005 of YouTube. YouTube is now one of the most popular and the largest website on the internet, with more than 2 billion active monthly users who watch billions of videos every day. How did this simple video-sharing site become so popular? Take a look back at YouTube's history and see what factors made it a worldwide phenomenon.

The Beginnings of YouTube

In February 2005, Chad Hurley (former CEO), Steve Chen (former CTO) and Jawed Khanim, all ex-PayPal employees, came together to create YouTube. The idea behind it was born when they struggled to find an easy way of sharing video footage from a dinner with their friends. They identified the absence of a simple online platform for sharing videos which led them to launch YouTube.

In November 2005, YouTube gained its initial momentum with the upload of a video called "Me at the Zoo." The video was uncomplicated and featured a man sharing his thoughts on elephants. However, it became incredibly popular and contributed significantly to establishing YouTube as a prime location for captivating and engaging videos. Subsequently, over the following months, YouTube attracted an immense user base that produced numerous viral videos.

YouTube's Early Challenges

YouTube's rapid growth was not without its challenges. Copyright violations were one of YouTube's biggest problems. Users were uploading music and videos that had copyrights which led to lawsuits between media companies and record label. YouTube was also struggling with lack of income since the platform was free and relying on advertising to generate revenue. YouTube made a series of platform changes to address the challenges. One of these was Content ID. This system allowed for copyright holders and media companies to identify, flag, and monetise videos that violated their rights (experimentation and innovation). YouTube also signed deals to license content from media companies, record labels and other content providers. This helped establish YouTube as an official destination for video content of high quality (ecosystem).

With its user-generated content strategy, it quickly established itself as the leading video-sharing platform (strategy). By providing a platform for users to upload and share their own videos, YouTube created a sense of community and engagement that helped to drive its growth (co-creation).

The Rise of YouTube as a Global Powerhouse

YouTube's people strategy played a significant role in its success. Attracting and retaining top talent was key for YouTube. It achieved this by providing employees with a creative, collaborative, and supportive work environment. The company also offered competitive compensation packages, opportunities for professional growth and development, and a supportive culture that fostered innovation and creativity (People).

YouTube has been known to practice lean and agile methodologies, particularly in its product development process. It focused on creating a Minimum Viable Product (MVP) as quickly as possible and then iterating and improving based on user feedback. This approach allowed YouTube to quickly test and validate new features and functionality and make changes based on user feedback (Lean). YouTube was also quick respond to changing market conditions and user needs, and to make rapid improvements to its platform. (Agile).

YouTube's adoption of technology played a crucial role in its triumph, as it facilitated swift and effective expansion of the platform while personalising user experience. Furthermore, it allowed YouTube to stay ahead in an ever-evolving digital environment (Technology). Some of its key technological adoptions were:

Adoption of video technology – YouTube, as an early adopter in video technology, was able leverage the technology to provide a smooth user experience when watching videos and sharing them. This investment included the development of codecs, playback technology and the infrastructure required to support massive video sharing.

Use of cloud computing – By utilising cloud computing, YouTube was able to expand its infrastructure and accommodate its fast-paced expansion. The company could allocate resources as necessary through cloud services, ultimately minimising expenses by paying solely for the computing resources utilised.

Investment in machine learning and artificial intelligence – By making significant investments in machine learning and artificial intelligence, YouTube was able to enhance its user experience through platform personalisation. This involved the utilisation of algorithms for video recommendations, transcription and captioning services, as well as identification and removal of inappropriate content (technology and constant reinvention).

Focus on mobile – YouTube acknowledged the increasing significance of mobile and prioritised enhancing its platform for mobile devices. This encompassed creating mobile applications, boosting video playback efficiency on such gadgets, and guaranteeing that their website was optimised to cater to mobile viewing.

With the remarkable growth of YouTube, it captured the attention of key players in the tech sector. In November 2006, Google declared its decision to purchase YouTube for an impressive $1.65 billion, ultimately strengthening its influence as a dominating force worldwide.

After being acquired by Google, YouTube underwent further growth and development as it rolled out various novel features and services aimed at improving user satisfaction. Among these were the launch of YouTube Partners which enabled users to earn income from their video content, the debut of YouTube TV – a streaming platform that offers both live and on-demand television programming, the introduction of music-centric portal called YouTube Music with millions of songs available alongside accompanying videos, along with gaming-focused channel named YouTube Gaming comprising live feeds as well as pre-recorded videos for gamers (constant reinvention & new business model).

Nowadays, YouTube holds a significant position among the most extensive and impactful online platforms globally. With more than two billion users engaging every month and an excess of one billion hours spent viewing videos each day, it has transformed into a vast hub for both entertainment and knowledge-sharing. This has attracted some of the world's most renowned creators and producers to showcase their content on this platform.

Conclusion

The progress of YouTube from a basic video-sharing platform to an international phenomenon has been truly extraordinary. Despite facing initial difficulties and hindrances, the platform has persevered in expanding and developing, enticing countless users, and revolutionising our approach towards producing and viewing videos. At present, YouTube is an indispensable aspect of our internet activities as it offers limitless opportunities for entertainment, learning, and motivation.

HISTORY OF YOUTUBE

HERE ARE THE MAJOR MILESTONE OF YOUTUBE THROUGHOUT THE YEARS

2005
YouTube's trademark, logo, and domain were registered
Site's first video was uploaded
Nike's video received its first million views

2006
Started its Content Verification Program after a copyright violation claim by NBC
Google purchased Youtube for $1.65 billion

2007
YouTube starts its Partner Program for individual content creators

2011
YouTube Live is launched

2012
Gagnam Style becomes first video with a billion views

2015
YouTube Red launch

2016-18
- YouTube Go debuts
- YouTube Red becomes YouTube Premium.
- YouTube ad pod testing.

2020
- YouTube launches Video Reach.
- YouTube eliminates categories.

2022
YouTube is the second-most popular social network globally.

VdoCipher

CREDITS

Christophe Bacon, Founder & Managing Director at Omnistrada

About Omnistrada - https://www.omnistrada.com/

Passionate about digital, we elaborate and deliver Digital and OmniChannel strategies that transform existing businesses or develop new business opportunities. At OmniStrada, we work with business owners, the c-suite and the rest of the management team, to articulate, plan and execute pragmatic and tactical Digital Transformation and OmniChannel strategies; whilst addressing organisational and local market challenges and realities.

OmniStrada was built around a cohesive team of proven business builders with compelling records of delivery. Our experience reflects a unique combination of skill sets that incorporate strategic planning, technical savvy and deep operational know-how allowing to address all key aspects and deliverables of successful digital transformation and omnichannel strategies.

Nur Hamurcu, Managing Director at &samhoud Asia

About &Samhoud - https://www.samhoudconsultancy.com/

The key to the success of organisations lies in human behaviour. Nevertheless, leaders often seek the solution to strategic questions in organisational changes, systems and processes. While the key question is, 'What human behaviour is desired to increase business opportunities and reduce risk?' This requires an unusual approach. An approach in which in-depth knowledge of the business and behaviour is combined. An approach that inspires and connects.

Based upon this philosophy we help our clients solving strategic challenges, while contributing to our higher goal, 'Together we build a brighter future. We achieve breakthroughs by inspiring and connecting people.'

Agata Bas, Customer Growth and Digital Experiences Expert

Agata Bas is an expert in customer growth and digital experiences, with a proven track record of developing customer-centric strategies that drive business growth. With her experience in digital marketing, brand experience, and customer retention, Agata has helped businesses achieve long-term success by transforming their brand and customer experiences. She formerly served as the Director of Creative Experience and Commerce at Dentsu, spearheading creative commerce solutions and innovations across various industries in Malaysia. Agata has also led teams focused on customer growth and digital experiences for Zalora across Southeast Asia and Mindvalley globally.

She is now advising startups and entrepreneurs on digital strategy and customer growth direction. She holds two Master's Degrees in Business Management and Psychology in Business, with a particular passion for the latter. She is obsessed with understanding customer behaviors, motives, and expectations, and creating ways to exceed them.

https://www.linkedin.com/in/agata-bas-42766069

ABOUT THE AUTHOR

Jheeva is a commercially focused business executive with 23 years of experience with multi-channel and multi-site retail and wholesale organisations within the luxury products industry. Jheeva started off his professional career in London with an accountancy firm before moving to the Radisson Edwardian Hotel Group. Jheeva moved into retail in 2006 with Agent Provocateur and then to Perfumers 1870 which operates the Penhaligons and L'Artisan Parfumeur brands. Having successfully restructured and help grow the brands globally as their Group Finance Director, Jheeva managed the sale of the brands to the Puig group before joining Puig as their Finance Director for Asia Pacific in Singapore, where he helped set up a partnership agreement with Clarins Australia to set up a Puig Subsidiary in Sydney and a joint venture deal with Luxasia in Singapore. At BHG Singapore as their CFO, Jheeva led their Finance, IT, Marketing, E-commerce and Digital Transformation functions. Currently Jheeva is the CEO of Protinus Group, which provides consultancy and direction from a business driven technology point of view to create new business models and new revenue streams.

https://www.linkedin.com/in/jheeva-subramanian-ab4349a/

ABOUT PROTINUS GROUP

Protinus Group is a digital transformation consultancy that works with companies to help them transform by using technology, improving processes, identifying new business models and revenue streams.

At Protinus, we believe divergent views at the outset of a project help us peel away the non-essential distractions. This helps us solve complex problems with clarity of thought. This singular-focused approach ensures we challenge the norm and ask the hard questions that enable us to create breakthrough solutions for brands and organisations.

The company's services include strategy development, digital transformation, technology implementation, operational improvement and strategic partnerships.

With a team of experts and a strong commitment to quality, Protinus Group helps clients improve their business operations and achieve their goals.

https://www.protinusgrp.com/

Transform your business with this essential guide to business transformation. This book offers practical advice and insights on how to stay ahead in today's fast-paced and ever-changing business world. Beginning with the importance of transformation and experimentation, the book goes on to explore the critical role of technology and the Platform as a business model.

People are at the centre of transformation, the Lean & Agile approach, co-creation, and ecosystems are explored in-depth. Chapter 9 offers practical advice on crafting a successful transformation strategy, followed by Chapter 10's exploration of new business models.

The book emphasises the need for constant reinvention to stay ahead, with Chapter 12 offering a glimpse into the future of business transformation. With an example of a Real Life Transformation Strategy for a Retail Company and a Case Study, this book is a must-read for any business leader looking to drive transformation and achieve success.

Jheeva Subramanian